THE CAPITAL MARKET:
ITS NATURE AND SIGNIFICANCE

STUDIES IN FINANCE AND ACCOUNTING

General Editors: M. J. Barron and D. W. Pearce

Published

Michael Firth: MANAGEMENT OF WORKING CAPITAL
Kenneth Midgley and Ronald Burns: THE CAPITAL MARKET: ITS NATURE AND SIGNIFICANCE

Forthcoming

M. J. Barron: BUSINESS FINANCE THEORY
M. J. Barron: MATRIX MODELS FOR ACCOUNTING
Michael Firth: THE VALUATION OF SHARES AND THE EFFICIENT-MARKETS THEORY
Brian Quinn: MULTINATIONAL BUSINESS FINANCE AND ACCOUNTING
T. Ryan: PORTFOLIO ANALYSIS
R. W. Scapens: ACCOUNTING IN AN INFLATIONARY ENVIRONMENT
Charles Sutcliffe: ECONOMICS VERSUS ACCOUNTANCY

The Capital Market:
its Nature and Significance

KENNETH MIDGLEY B.A., B.Sc.(Econ.), Ph.D., F.C.I.S.

Principal Lecturer in Finance, Brighton Polytechnic

and

RONALD BURNS M.Phil., A.C.C.A.

Senior Lecturer in Business Studies, Portsmouth Management Centre, Portsmouth Polytechnic

M

First published 1977 by
THE MACMILLAN PRESS LTD
London and Basingstoke
Associated companies in New York Dublin
Melbourne Johannesburg and Madras

ISBN 0 333 17437 2 (hard cover)
0 333 21486 2 (paper cover)

Typeset, printed and bound
in Great Britain by
REDWOOD BURN LIMITED
Trowbridge & Esher

Contents

General Editors' Preface

The last few years have been very exciting for research in finance and accounting. An enormous amount has happened, and in many cases traditional thinking and traditional solutions have been completely overthrown. At the same time it is quite clear that research into the theory and, perhaps even more important, into British empirical evidence, will continue to accumulate rapidly. While this is fine for the researcher in his detailed specialist world, it is not so good for the student who wants to acquire a relatively straightforward but up-to-date overview of the subject.

The 'Macmillan Studies in Finance and Accounting' set out to provide short, reasonably critical surveys of the developments within the various specialist areas of business finance and accounting. The emphasis in each study is upon recent work, but each topic will generally be placed in a historical context so that the reader may see the logical development of thought through time. Selected bibliographies are provided to guide readers to more extensive works. Each study aims at a brief treatment of the salient problems in order to avoid clouding the issues in too much detailed argument.

Unfortunately it is inevitable that in a few areas the level of mathematics will be rather near the limit for some students. This is because the rigorous methods of statistics, econometrics and mathematical economics have made a considerable contribution to the research achievements in the subject. Thus, although all the authors in the series have tried hard to make their presentation as lucid as possible there is a point beyond which mathematical arguments cannot be explained non-mathematically except at a superficial level. Nevertheless intuition can go a long way and many students, even with very little mathematical background, have found that the intrinsic fascination of the subject more than compensates for occasional difficulty.

M. J. Barron
D. W. Pearce

CHAPTER 1

The Role of the Capital Market and the Purposes which it Serves

A market provides a focus for the activities of buyers and sellers of a particular commodity or service. In the course of the dealings the price or series of prices is settled. The participants in the U.K. capital market include businessmen, central and local government, financial intermediaries such as insurance companies and pension funds, and private investors. The capital market has no confined location: it is in progress all over the land, wherever suppliers and users of capital get together to do business. Much business is transacted over the telephone, so that there need be no geographical site at all for certain activities. However, *parts* of the market are concentrated in certain well-known centres, the most renowned of these being the Stock Exchange at Throgmorton Street which deals in company securities and those issued by governments and local authorities.

The capital market deals in funds, but as securities, for example bonds or share certificates, are given in exchange for funds, one can equally treat it as a market dealing in securities. The market conforms to the laws of supply and demand in the ordinary way. Thus if the demand for funds increases and the supply remains constant (or contracts) the price of funds rises (that is, the price of securities falls). If the demand for funds contracts and supply remains constant (or increases) the price of funds falls (that is, the price of securities rises).

Within the capital market one can speak of the price of funds in a general way, just as in the fish market one can speak of the price of fish. But of course nobody buys just *fish*; one does not ask for a pound (or kilogram, to be more up to date) of fish, but rather a pound of cod, or a kilo of haddock. Similarly, in the capital market the buyers of funds are in practice specific about their requirements. They may wish to raise £1 million of risk capital, or £500,000 of capital on long-term loan, or £200,000 on bank overdraft, and so on.

The price paid for access to funds may be in the form of a fixed payment per annum (though it may be paid in instalments, for example, twice a year) or it may be in the form of an agreement to share profits. An example of the former circumstance is where interest is paid to providers of loan capital; and the latter circumstance is exemplified where dividends are paid out to shareholders. (However, we must hasten to add that shareholders are not rewarded only by dividend payments: if that were the case some companies would appear to be giving a meagre return to risk capital. Part of the return to shareholders is in the form of retained earnings which augment the capital of the company and thereby make possible the expansion of future earnings. Potential growth in earnings is a factor taken into consideration by the market, and if it is regarded as sufficiently attractive the share price will rise so as to reflect this expected future growth.)

The student of finance will probably find it useful at this point to reflect on factors generally which could influence the cost of capital funds, or, the reciprocal, the price of securities. Perhaps one of the first influences which will come to mind is the extent of funds available from public savings. Another fairly obvious influence is the level of demand for funds arising from plans for new forms of industrial and commercial investment. These will provide a starting point, but in practice there are many complex factors which exert their influence on the market. On the supply side there is of course the flow of funds stemming from the banking system. An easy credit policy which leads to the creation of new bank money will lead, *ceteris paribus*, to a reduction in the cost of funds. Bank credit policy, however, will not be unrelated to governmental fiscal policy; for example, a budget deficit financed by issue of short-term securities may encourage expansion of bank credit and thus lower the cost of funds.

In its turn governmental fiscal policy will not be immune to the behaviour of the balance of payments and capital movements in and out of the country. A serious run-down of a country's reserves of foreign currencies will almost certainly be countered by fiscal stringency and credit restrictions leading to an increase in the cost of capital.

One of the most cogent influences on the cost of funds is the attitude to liquidity on the part of investors as a whole. (The stock market meaning of the word 'investors', that is people, institutions, etc. who purchase securities, is used here.) If investors decide that the return to funds which they provide is too low, or in other words the price of securities is too high, there may be a sudden and overwhelming desire to hold cash or near-cash for the time being. This may result in a fairly rapid slump in security prices, or, the same thing, an increase in the return to funds, that is in the cost of capital. Conversely, investors may decide that they are too liquid and that returns to funds are too attractive to ignore. For example, it was known that the institutional investors (insurance companies, pension funds, investment trusts and unit trusts) were holding large liquid balances towards the end of 1974. Once security prices began to rise in January 1975, and investors began to appreciate that the return to funds provided was falling, they flooded the market for securities with buying orders to such a degree that the *Financial Times* Actuaries All Share Index rose by over 100 per cent within a few weeks. Looking at this dramatic change from the point of view of the return to funds, the earnings yield on industrial ordinary shares fell from over 30 per cent to 20 per cent within a month. The flat yield on Consols (that is a general indication of the return on long-term giltedged securities) also fell during this short period, though by no means so spectacularly, from 16 per cent to less than 15 per cent.

In fact, different sectors of the market for securities are subject to different influences. The returns to funds in different sectors may move more or less rapidly over time, as noted above. It is possible too that the returns in one sector may be rising when the returns to other sectors are falling. Thus long-term fixed interest rates may be rising when short-term rates are falling; or the earnings yield on industrial shares generally may be falling when that on, say, engineering shares is rising. Generally though, apart from occasional exceptional moves against the trend, the returns in different broad sectors of the market move together in the same direction, though not at the same pace. This is illustrated in the Figure 1.1.

The more one focuses attention on narrow sectors of the market, the more likely it is that one will come across areas which 'buck the trend' or at least drag a long way behind the general movement. To refer to the fish-market analogy once again, while the general trend in fish prices may be upwards at a particular time, it is not unlikely that on a particular day the price of a particular type of fish, say locally caught bream, may move down because of a good catch.

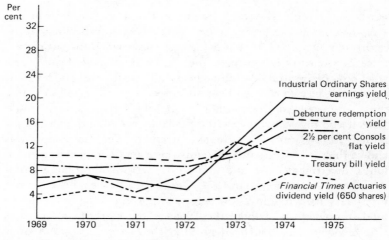

Source: *Financial Statistics* (December 1975)

Figure 1.1   *Trends in interest rates/yields*

Similarly, when share prices generally are moving in a particular direction, it is often the case that the shares of a particular sector are moving in the opposite direction. Gold-mine shares, during many months of 1974, were rising, in spite of the general slump in most other share prices.

It is not then sufficient merely to examine factors affecting demand and supply for funds generally. Rather one must look at factors affecting particular industries and, of course, particular firms. The more one concentrates attention on particular firms, the more specialised are the influences which must be examined. If the Fidelity Fiduciary Insurance Company is able to borrow funds at a lower rate than the Go Go Growth Insurance Company, such factors as calibre of management, asset holdings, gearing ratio, recent past performance and future prospects will have to be compared in order to ascertain the likely causes of the disparity.

It may help the student's understanding at this stage if some of the factors which influence the cost of funds, generally and in particular sections of the market, are grouped together, with an indication of their likely effects on price(s). This is done in Table 1.1. The items listed are not exhaustive and each effect is examined on the assumption that other influences remain undisturbed (though in practice of

Table 1.1

Factors affecting the cost of funds/price(s) of securities

Factors leading to *general* fund/security price changes

| Changes in demand for funds | Expansion/contraction of industrial and commercial investment leading to increased/reduced level of issues of securities
Increased/lowered level of company taxation, lowered/increased profit retentions, leading to increased/reduced level of issues
Increased/reduced level of government spending leading to increases/reductions of issues of government securities
Overall budget deficit/surplus whereby government finances its expenditure to a lesser/greater extent from taxation as opposed to capital issues
Reduced/increased liquidity preference of investors |
| Changes in supply of funds | Contraction/expansion of bank credit
Reduced/increased level of savings
Increased/reduced liquidity preference of investors
Outflow/inflow of funds to/from abroad |

Factors leading to fund/security price changes *within an industry*

| Changes in demand for funds | General expansion, direct and/or via mergers
Contraction within the industry
Less/greater reliance on retained profits
Increased level of innovation, discoveries or invention |
| Changes in supply of funds | Lack of confidence by investors in the future of the industry
Enthusiasm for the future of the industry on the part of investors reflected in increased purchase of 'second-hand' securities and willingness to subscribe for new issues |

---

course a change in one factor may trigger off or be associated with changes in other factors) and that the general level of activity remains unchanged. The net effect of a combination of various factors will depend on their relative strengths and directions. The movement generally in the price of funds at any particular time will be particularly subject to the liquidity preference of investors; and investors are apt to be looking a year or so ahead in making their decisions. Consequently, investors' views as to the desirability of holding cash or near-cash as against the alternative of holding securities may sometimes appear to run contrary to other economic indicators. For example, in spite of a rapidly increasing level of industrial production, falling unemployment, and a steady increase in the supply of money in the first six months of 1973, the general level of security prices began the long downward spiral which ended in January 1975 with the *Financial Times* Actuaries All Share Index at about a third of its level in January 1973, and, in the fixed-interest sector, the flat yield on irredeemable gilt-edged securities up from 10 per cent in January 1973 to 17 per cent by January 1975.

The reader will probably have understood from previous remarks that the prices of funds (or securities) are by no means dependent on new savings in relation to new industrial investment. The new securities issued at any particular time are paltry in amount compared with the total amount of 'second-hand' securities (that is those issued in previous months and years). Thus important changes in the liquidity preference of investors (that is in favour of holding more or less securities), which are largely reflected in purchases or sales of the existing huge stock of second-hand securities, are often mainly responsible for the cyclical swings in security prices and prices of funds.

Turning now to an area within the general market for funds, we can look at some factors operating on an industrial sector. Here it is even more important to emphasise that the effects suggested above only apply if other factors remain unchanged. Thus an increased demand for funds arising from discoveries of, say, oil, will raise the rates of return offered to investors in the securities of that industry, assuming no change in the supply of funds. In practice it may well be the case that the new prospects open to the industry excite investors to a point that they move funds massively into this industrial sector, thus swamping and reversing the effect of an increase in the demand for funds.

So far we have spoken very generally about the rate of returns to funds. In attempting to simplify the concept of the capital market we must not, however, ignore some of the complexities. We have seen that the market can be sub-divided into industrial sectors and that funds are offered and required on different terms. Now we must examine in more detail the different types of security offered for funds.

Securities can be viewed in terms of the varying rates of risk involved for the supplier of funds. As a general rule the more safe and sure the investment, the lower the rate of return that can be expected. The safety of an investment depends broadly on the security offered, if any, the standing of the issuing body and the duration of the arrangement – the longer one has to wait for repayment, the greater the risk that the supplier of the funds will suffer from inconvenience or dissatisfaction in the settlement. Not least of the difficulties is that arising from inflation, that is to say, that the real value of the repayment monies is much depleted compared with the real value of the sum lent. (Some of the problems arising from inflation are dealt with at a later point. Funds provided on an irredeemable basis are generally subject to the greatest risk. Such funds can either be provided subject to a fixed-interest agreement, or subject to an agreement that the supplier shall be entitled to a certain share of the profit, as in the case of equity shares in a limited company.

The main types of 'fund contract', or securities, are set out broadly in order of risk in Table 1.2. The table is by no means comprehensive, but it provides an indication of the risk spectrum to be discussed. If the securities are listed roughly in order of risk, it may be expected that the returns to the suppliers of funds will be in similar order, that is greatest return to equities, next greatest to preference shares, and so on, and least to very short-term securities. There are reasonable grounds for this expectation, but for technical reasons there may occasionally be disparities within the spectrum. A particular difficulty in any attempt to support this view of varying returns with figures is that the return to ordinary shares, that is the dividend plus any capital gain, is obviously subject to variation. Furthermore, the figures available refer to the dividend and earnings yields of the *previous* accounting year – not to the *expected* yield during the forthcoming year. A moment's thought will persuade the reader that the *expected* return to the shareholder must be higher than that on any fixed-interest security. There is no certainty of a dividend in the case of a shareholding, and, moreover, the share price is liable to fluctuate considerably. Thus an investor, who can get a certain yield of 14 per cent on a fixed-interest security is unlikely to invest, say £1000, in an ordinary share with a probable dividend of £80 unless he expects a capital gain on his holding over the year of at least £61 (giving an over-all yield of 14·1 per cent, ignoring tax).

Subject to this important provision regarding the unreliability of past earnings as a guide to *expected* return, the graph in Figure 1.1

Table 1.2

Classes of security	Examples of types of contract	Fund-raisers
Equities	Various types of ordinary share (voting/non-voting)	Limited companies
Preference shares	Cumulative Non-cumulative Redeemable	,, ,,
Debentures	Convertible Non-convertible	,, ,,
Fixed interest Irredeemable	Government stock (e.g. 3½ per cent War Loan)	Government
Long-term (15 years +)	Government stock (e.g. Gas 3 per cent 1990–5)	Governments (central and local)
Medium-term (5–15 years)	Government stock (e.g. Treasury 5 per cent 1986–9)	,, ,,
Short-term (up to 5 years)	Bank loans (if fixed interest) Commercial bills Government stocks etc. (e.g. Treasury Stock 11½ per cent 1979)	Governments, firms
Variable interest	Bank loans and overdrafts Building Society mortgage accounts	Firms, individuals and governments

(p. 4) gives a fair degree of confirmation of the view that risky and longer-term securities offer the highest return.

Before leaving this aspect of the capital market a little more attention must be given to the impact of inflation on rates of return. The fact that the rate of inflation has gradually accelerated over the decade up to 1975, and the fact that rates of return have risen over the years, is no coincidence. The U.K. rates of inflation are set out in Table 1.3. The general average of rates of return does not necessarily vary in direct proportion to the rate of inflation. It might be thought, for example, that if, with stable prices, the centre of the spectrum of interest rates would be about 5 per cent, then with a rate of inflation of 10 per cent (that is, involving a loss to holders of

Table 1.3

General index of retail prices (Percentage increase on year earlier)	
1968	4·7
1969	5·4
1970	6·4
1971	9·4
1972	7·1
1973	9·2
1974	16·1
1975	24·9

Source: *Economic Trends* (January 1976).

interest-bearing securities who are repaid with money which is losing value each year at the rate of 10 per cent) the interest rate would have to be 15 per cent; similarly, with an inflation rate of 20 per cent the interest rate would have to be 25 per cent. In fact, at the time of writing (mid-1975), though a rate of inflation of 25 per cent is being experienced, the rate of interest to be gained by investing in long-term government securities is only about 14 per cent; in other words the investor apparently stands to lose up to 10 per cent of the value of his money (before taking tax into account) in terms of current purchasing power! What is the explanation for this phenomenon? Probably the main reason is that investors, realising that the government is under pressure to deal with the balance-of-payments deficit, expect firm action to reduce the rate of inflation. If the inflation level is expected to be halved by the end of the year, it becomes more logical to invest at 14 per cent. Furthermore, if future interest rates are expected to fall because of a reduction in the rate of inflation, prospective borrowers will try to avoid borrowing long term, so that the lack of demand for the long-term funds in such circumstances will help to bring down the long-term rate of interest. A further point is that in times of inflation it becomes difficult to find any safe haven for money. Investment in gold, pictures, antiques, etc. carries its own risk. Investment with a 14 per cent return, even if negative after taking inflation into account, is better than no money return at all. Yet a further point is that investors need to keep some funds in reasonably liquid form. High rates of inflation mean that people need to have larger money balances readily available for transactions and precautionary purposes. Thus some money must be available without too much difficulty. Some forms of investment, for example property, may take months to realise. Investment in *market* securities can, however, be turned back into cash (though possibly at some loss) within days rather than months. This last point will be taken up again in discussing the advantages of a market for securities in the last section of this chapter.

Reasons for the Issue of Different Types of Security/Terms of Funds Supply

From the point of view of suppliers of funds it is easy to understand how a demand arises for different types of security. Some people have funds which they can spare for only a very short time; others are prepared to supply funds more or less permanently in return for a certain income (annuities for example); others are prepared to supply funds only if they are given terms of absolute security; others do not mind parting with funds in risky circumstances if the prospective rewards are large enough.

The mere fact that suppliers of funds have varying tastes in securities does not in itself explain the issue of a variety of types of security; no more in fact than the knowledge on the part of a greengrocer that the public generally has a wide-ranging taste for fruit explains the variety in the produce offered. In both cases demand will be met only if it is profitable to do so. Usually, however, this will be so. Thus, if a greengrocer filled his shop with oranges and nothing else, he may find that, to clear his stocks, he would have to offer oranges at a price below that which he paid, or at any rate at a price which would give him little profit. Similarly, if a large organisation taps only one source of funds supply, it will not get the most favourable terms. For example, if the government issued only irredeemable securities in order to raise all funds needed, it would have to pay a very high price indeed for its borrowing. Many potential suppliers of funds are simply not in that section of the market. But the government is well aware that by tapping all sources of supply – the gamblers (premium bonds), the tax-avoiders (national savings certificates), the play-safers (short-term loans), the specialist money-lenders (treasury bills), those who demand inflation-proof contracts (S.A.Y.E.), and so on – the finance needs of the government are met as cheaply as possible. Similarly, companies may find that they can lower the average cost of funds raised by approaching different suppliers: lenders against security (for example, issues of debentures), semi-risk-takers with a fixed maximum rate of return, and risk-takers who take the surplus earned.

Companies have a special reason for gearing up by issue of loan capital: loan capital interest is treated as a cost which reduces the taxable profits. Thus, with corporation tax at 52 per cent, if money had to be borrowed at 20 per cent, the true cost, after taking into account that 52 per cent of the interest charge is a tax reduction, is 48 per cent of 20 per cent, that is 9·6 per cent. Similarly, the true cost, if money could be borrowed at 10 per cent, would be 48 per cent of 10 per cent, that is 4·8 per cent. An example is shown in Table 1.4.

Table 1.4

Trading profit before interest charge:	if interest allowed as deduction for taxable profits	if interest not so allowed
	(£) 100,000	(£) 100,000
Less gross interest (say)	10,000	
	90,000	
Less corporation tax @ 52 per cent	46,800	52,000
		48,000
		10,000
Difference (tax-saving) = £5200 (that is 52 per cent of £10,000)	43,200	38,000

Raising funds by issue of preference shares is not quite so attractive from the point of view of a company. Nevertheless the true cost to the company of preference dividends is effectively reduced by the current imputation tax system, as the standard income tax rate on the dividend is treated as having been paid when it is received by the shareholder. Consequently, with an income tax rate of 35 per cent, a company can pay a dividend worth £10,000 gross (that is if it had been subject to income tax) in the hands of the shareholder at a cost to itself of only £6500. The true cost to the company of a preference dividend is therefore only 65 per cent of its gross value. Moreover, there is a special demand for preference shares from institutions such as insurance companies and investment trusts, for preference dividends are treated as franked income in their hands; that is to say, it is recognised that they have been paid out of profits which have already suffered corporation tax and therefore they are exempt (franked) from any further corporation tax in the hands of these institutions. This advantage, by the way, does not apply to debenture interest, for, as we have already seen, this escapes corporation tax, and thus is not franked.

Table 1.5

£'000	Company X		Company Y	
Equity capital and Reserves	400		200	
15 per cent Debenture stock	100		300	
(a)				
Appropriation of profits (before interest deductible) of 75 = to 15 per cent of total capital:				
debenture holders	15		45	
		% of equity		*% of equity*
ordinary shareholders	60	15	30	15
(b)				
Appropriation of profits of 100:				
debenture holders	15		45	
ordinary shareholders	85	21·25	55	27·5
(c)				
Appropriation of profits of 50:				
debenture holders	15		45	
ordinary shareholders	35	8·75	5	2·5

Clearly, there are certain advantages to both suppliers and users of funds in the issue of securities on a variety of terms. Nevertheless, from a company's point of view, it must be appreciated that the use of fixed-interest issues in gearing up the capital employed imposes a degree of risk on top of that already borne by companies in the very nature of their being. Consider the example shown in Table 1.5 illustrating the effect of different degrees of gearing at different profit levels. Both companies are assumed to earn similar returns to total capital employed in each instance, and, for the sake of simplicity, taxation is ignored.

It is seen that if the company can earn no more on its capital than it pays to its lenders as in (*a*), there is neither gain nor loss to equity holders because of the gearing. If the company can earn more on its capital than it pays to its lenders (as in (*b*)), there is an increase in the percentage return available to equity holders – the higher the gearing, the greater the increase. But if the company earns less on its total capital than it pays to its lenders (as in (*c*)), there is a reduction in the percentage return available to equity holders – the higher the gearing in such cases, the greater the reduction.* Indeed, if the company earnings fall badly enough or become negative there will be an over-all loss (or negative return) to the equity interest. Consider the situation, for example, in the case of company Y if profit before interest charge fell to £25,000. Using the formula

$$ER = p + \frac{D}{E} (p - i), \text{ we get } 5 + \frac{3}{2} (5 - 15) = -10 \text{ per cent}$$

(that is a net loss of £20,000 for an equity interest of £200,000).

The above illustrations indicate that while companies find it to their advantage to issue one or other form of fixed-interest security, there are obvious risk limitations to this process.

Yet another consideration which has a bearing on the nature of securities issued by a company is the natural desire on the part of those who are in control of a company's affairs to maintain that control. It is not usually necessary in practice for a founder of a business or his successors to retain over 50 per cent of the equity for this purpose.[2] A holding of as little as 10 per cent of the voting shares will often be adequate where the rest of the shares are well spread.

---

* The net effective return to equity holders where gearing is made use of can be calculated using the following formula:

$$ER = p + \frac{D}{E} (p - i),$$

where ER = return to equity, P = return to *all* capital in use including borrowed funds after tax, i = interest rate on debt, D = 'debt' (funds raised on fixed-interest terms), E = equity capital. (*ER* is also the maximum growth rate.)[1]

However, as the proportionate holdings of the controllers diminish as the company becomes larger, there may well be some increasing reluctance to raise funds in a manner which undermines the privileged position of those in control. A satisfactory means of fund-raising in such circumstances, from the point of view of the controllers, has been the issue of shares with restricted voting rights. These impose no additional risk on existing shareholders, as the holders of such shares generally take no priority over voting share-holders in the division of profit. Such shares have been frowned on by company-law reformists,[3] and it seems quite probable that they will be prohibited by the terms of future legislation. An alternative way of raising funds without at the same time over-extending control is to be found in the issue of preference shares, which, though subject to the internal rules of the company, do not normally carry voting rights unless the dividend is in arrear.

To sum up this section, we can say that a wide choice of securities is available in the market for funds because: (*a*) by tapping each potential source of supply of funds, the users of funds, including central government, local government and business, obtain them at the lowest possible cost; (*b*) certain securities have special advantages in terms of current taxation regulations and are thus favoured; (*c*) fixed-interest securities have a particular attraction for companies, for in so far as the company can earn a better return on the total capital it uses than the rate of interest it pays on borrowed capital, it can increase the net return to equity capital, or, in other words, it can enhance its potential growth rate; and (*d*) the consideration of control of the company has a bearing on the type of securities which are issued to promote the further expansion of a company.

The Functions of the Capital Market

The fact that the capital market, or at least that part of it represented by the Stock Exchange, is sometimes regarded as providing a service not unlike that of a casino does not mean that it has no important, sober and useful functions. Like any other market, the capital market provides a means whereby suppliers and buyers can exchange a commodity at mutually satisfactory prices. Here lies perhaps the most obvious, and certainly the most important, of the market's functions: that of creating liquidity. Were it not for the market most of the longer-term securities issued by companies would be far more permanent investments in the hands of their holders. Without an organised market, the owner of a block of ordinary shares in a particular company who wished to dispose of his holding would have to make a personal search for a potential buyer. He may have to advertise and/or employ an agent; he may have to suffer the inconvenience of a considerable delay before finally finding a buyer, and the price agreed upon would almost certainly be much less satisfactory than that settled in an organised market where many buyers and sellers confront each other. Without the market-endowed quality of liquidity, company shares and debentures would be far less attractive to investors, and companies would have difficulty in raising all the funds they needed for expansion. It is of course true that a comparatively small part of company funds are raised externally from investors at present, but this part may nevertheless be of vital importance. Consequently, the liquidity provided by the stock market (in particular) serves the very useful purpose of ensuring that external investors are willing to make new funds available to business as required.

The market not only creates liquidity through its pricing mechanism, it also allocates and rations funds, and it operates a system of incentives and penalties. As we have already seen, the market prices funds for borrowers and suppliers according to their different requirements. For large, efficient companies, which can offer sound securities subject to the minimum of risk, the rate for borrowing will be comparatively low. For smaller companies, which cannot give the same assurance of safety, the rate will be higher. Furthermore, the *shares* of a successful company with good growth prospects will be priced much higher in the market than those of a similar-sized company with a poor record and uncertain growth prospects. One effect of this is that potential growth companies in expanding industries tend to have much lower earnings and dividend yields than companies with uninspired management in declining industries. In short, the 'super-companies' can raise funds by equity share issues with the minimum immediate obligation in terms of cash outflow to the providers of capital (though of course the latter will be looking for rapid growth in future years); while the companies which lack investor confidence will issue securities subject to the maximum obligation in terms of annual cash returns to investors. The market is thus conferring a considerable advantage on the more efficient companies.[4] For them that hath, to them shall be given!

The market pricing of shares has further repercussion on companies other than its effect on the allocation of funds. Share-price movements operate so as to provide both sticks and carrots for those who manage quoted companies. The mechanisms are various. One fairly obvious form of discipline to management is that exercised by shareholders who are dissatisfied with the trend in the share price. For some, usually small quoted companies, the holdings of certain individual shareholders are sufficiently large for them to take direct action, such as removing directors from the board. In the case of larger companies, the holdings are often so widely spread that no individual, or group of individuals, holds sufficient shares to exercise power, and the directors, in such circumstances, although themselves holding only a small fraction of total voting shares, can retain full control in the absence of any concerted opposition.[5] This situation is not all-pervasive among large companies. Sometimes ginger groups are set up to act on behalf of the mass of individual shareholders. Moreover, in most large companies institutional shareholders now hold between one-third and one-half of the equity shares and via their separate investment protection committees or their combined institutional shareholders committee may act as a disciplining force. However, it has to be said that in spite of some notable successes, such forms of direct action tend to have been brought to bear too late to avoid the damage which they sought to avert.[6] This does not mean, incidentally, that shareholders must remain powerless in terms of direct influence; rather, it may be argued that more effective and permanent methods of representation must be forged.[7]

Share price movements frequently provide incentives and penalties on a personal basis for top managers of large companies. Many directors have large shareholdings,[8] and thus have a personal incentive to work to promote the efficiency of the company and hence upgrade the value of their own stake (and, inevitably, those of others) – and, of course, to avoid the penalty of a falling share price which could arise if they were slipshod in undertaking their role. Nowadays, even if managers have not the wealth to acquire a large holding of shares by direct personal investment, they may profit from share-incentive or stock-option schemes. Such schemes vary in detail according to the circumstances operative at the time of their introduction and are prone to the taxation policy of the government of the day. Fundamentally, the idea is that chosen directors and executives, who can influence the profitability of the company, are given the right to subscribe at some time in the future to the shares of their company, but at the current day's price. In this way they have a strong incentive to work for increased profits, which, if sufficiently meritorious in relation to results of other companies, will lead to a higher share price. Participants to the scheme can then exercise their options and sell their shares, thus enjoying a capital gain – the reward for their efforts. The scheme will be subject to various restrictions to avoid undue dilution of capital (that is an increase in share capital unsupported by a corresponding increase in net assets). For example, participants may be prevented from selling their shares within a stipulated period from allotment; there will be limitations to the total amount of shares issued under a scheme, and also to the shares issued to any individual; and/or a profit target may be built into the scheme, with the effect that participants can only gain if the target is achieved and other shareholders get some benefit from company growth. In Britain the introduction of stock-option schemes was encouraged by a House of Lords decision[9] that the taxable benefit of a share option was its value at the time it was exercised. Thus in the early 1960s an executive under a stock-option scheme was liable to income tax and surtax on the excess only of the value of the option over the price paid for it. This excess was likely to be a very small or even nil liability. When the option was exercised and the shares sold, the executive gained a capital profit free of tax. Such gains were brought into the income tax and surtax net by the 1966 Finance Act, which effectively curtailed this kind of incentive scheme (though not the more sophisticated schemes which emerged) until the 1972 Finance Act. This Act reinstated stock options subject to specified conditions.[10] Since that time the 1973–4 slump in share prices has meant that many schemes show little prospect of a profit for participants until the share price improves substantially.

Share-incentive schemes involved a consideration of which managers should be entitled to benefit and to what extent. Inevitably, the right will tend to be made available in relation to the degree of importance in the management hierarchy. This may mean that a particular executive who has made a substantial entrepreneurial contribution, but who is fairly low down in the hierarchy, is not adequately compensated by a share-incentive scheme. However, one means of compensation may be open to him, although it is a means which is generally frowned upon, that is, profiting from dealing in shares on the basis of inside knowledge. The arguments against this are fairly well known, although the practice, in a variety of forms, is probably less uncommon than some City apologists would care to admit.[11] Broadly, insider trading is said to put outsiders at a disadvantage, to allow insiders to profit at the expense of shareholders who are unaware of the inside information, and to undermine confidence on the part of the investing public. The extent of public disapproval of the practice is indicated in the clause to make insider trading a criminal offence in the lapsed 1973 Companies Bill.

Nevertheless, the case for insider trading as a means of rewarding the modern company entrepreneur has been cogently made.[12] It has been argued that because insider trading in company stocks does not suppress *long-term* trends, it does little harm to long-term outside investors. As for short-term outside speculators, such losses as they might make as a result of selling (or buying) before inside information becomes generally known would probably have been made anyway. More importantly though, it is argued that the possibility of dealing in the company's own shares provides incentives for anyone who makes an entrepreneurial contribution: that it can reward company entrepreneurs in a more precise manner than bonus or incentive schemes; that it rewards regardless of status, and yet ensures that *all* investors gain as well as entrepreneurs. Whether or not such arguments are given serious weight,[13] they do at least illustrate theoretically how company executives might be motivated to work harder and more imaginatively for the company in response to the possibility of making gains from share price movements stemming from their own efforts.

There are two more reasons for thinking that share price movements exert an influence on company management. One is that the share price barometer provides a rough and ready indicator of the success of company management. A share price which is falling more than those of rival companies (or not rising as fast) may be thought to cast a reflection on management efficiency, and managers are unlikely to be insensitive to the view that share price movements have a bearing on their competence.

If some thick-skinned managers are immune to the aspersions on their efficiency implicit in a falling share price, they may be more open to influence by a pressure more germane to their pockets and power positions than to their public image. Again, the pressure derives from share price movements, but here we refer to the view that the depressed share price of a company which has had a poor profits record will make it vulnerable to a takeover bid, and that the possibility of dismissal or reduced status and prospects may act as a spur to management to do better. (It will be appreciated that ordinary voting shares carry rights of control – if the shares become cheap, then control can be cheaply obtained.) However, it must be said that empirical evidence provides only meagre support for the proposition that a company which is relatively cheap in terms of the relationship between its equity stock market price and the book value of its equity assets (this latter being treated as an estimate of relative potential value) is in practice much more vulnerable to a takeover bid than a company which has a high valuation ratio of this sort.[14] (One practical difficulty facing a prospective bidder is that of deciding whether a poor profits record and low share price is the result of bad management or circumstances beyond a company's control. Another difficulty is that some firms are virtually invulnerable to a takeover bid because of their size. Who, other than the government, would have been prepared to bid for British Leyland?)[15] Even if the spur provided by falling share prices, and the possibility of takeover depends more on fear than fact for many companies, the stock market may still be exerting a useful influence favouring company efficiency.

To sum up, the capital market supports the whole basis of business undertaken by joint-stock limited companies. By providing a means of converting long-term investments into liquid funds, it gives a foundation of confidence to the process of saving and investment. The pricing process for securities not only leads to the allocation of funds to those companies which can make best use of them, it also provides penalties and incentives to managers, both directly and indirectly, and even threatens to operate through the takeover mechanism (that is, via the market for corporate control) to put the management of inefficient companies into more competent hands. How successfully these functions work or are impeded in practice will be a matter for discussion in later chapters, particularly in Chapter 6.

Further Reading

N. D. Berman, *The Stock Exchange* (London: Pitman, 1966).

R. J. Briston, *The Stock Exchange and Investment Analysis* (London: Unwin, 1975).

W. J. Baumol, *The Stock Market and Economic Efficiency* (New York: Fordham, 1965).

M. Gilbert, *The Modern Business Enterprise* (Harmondsworth: Penguin, 1972).

H. G. Manne, *Insider Trading and the Stock Market* (New York: The Free Press, 1966).

N. Macrae, *The London Capital Market* (London: Staples Press, 1957).

K. Midgley and R. G. Burns, *Business Finance and the Capital Market* (London: Macmillan, 1972).

G. D. Newbould, *Management and Merger Activity* (Liverpool: Guthstead, 1970).

J. F. Weston and E. F. Brigham, *Managerial Finance* (New York: Holt, 1975).

CHAPTER 2

The Fund-Raisers

In this chapter we concentrate our attention on the borrowers of money in this country: why they borrow money; the sources of the funds; and the amounts involved. Many of the features mentioned are referred to again in later chapters in more depth.

The Borrowers of Finance: An Introduction

Perhaps an easy way to start to appreciate the subject is to consider the personal financing of an individual. We will assume our 'guinea pig' earns an income and spends most of it on current or revenue expenditure. That part of his income which is not consumed we assume will be saved. It may be left on current account with his bank or, more likely, transferred to a deposit account or building society. We have here the rudiments of a financial system, namely, income, expenditure, savings and two financial institutions – a clearing bank and a building society.

Our friend may at some time in the future find that his relationship with these two institutions becomes reversed; he could easily become a borrower rather than a saver. For example, he may find that in a particular month he has expenditure in excess of his income. This could arise because an electricity bill and car insurance both have to be paid in the same month. His bank will quite likely allow him to overdraw his account providing that the imbalance between income and expenditure can be shown to be a temporary affair.

As far as the building society is concerned our friend may at some future time receive a loan with which to buy a house, on terms which involve future repayments of loan and interest over an extended period.

These two illustrations are examples of common reasons for

borrowing finance, namely a temporary imbalance between cash received and regular expenditure, and second the purchase of permanent or at any rate long-term assets. The second type of expenditure is known as 'capital expenditure'. Needless to say, only a minority of individuals have bank overdrafts, and furthermore much capital expenditure other than housing is financed directly from an individual's past savings rather than borrowing. Businesses, central government and local government will all find that their affairs sometimes involve the need to borrow for reasons similar to those described, and possibly for other reasons. In the course of borrowing they will encounter a variety of financial institutions.

At a *national level* we spend enormous sums on capital expenditure. The part of the *national* income spent this way, that is, on gross domestic fixed capital formation, totalled over £16,000 million in 1974 (see Table 2.13, p. 46 for an analysis by sector), and for the ten years 1963–72 on average slightly over 20 per cent of our gross domestic product was so spent. (In contrast, over much the same period Japan's gross investment as a percentage of G.D.P. averaged 34 per cent.)

Business Borrowings

You will recall that we have already suggested that businesses borrow money to finance a temporary imbalance between cash inflow into the business and cash outflow from it, and for the purchase of long-term assets – capital expenditure.

There is a further reason for business borrowings and that relates to a time lag between the receipts and payments associated with the trading cycle of a business. A business will incur wage costs and certain overhead costs (for example rent, rates, lighting and heating) at a very early stage in the sequence of events contributing to a business's trading cycle. Those events may be summarised as receipt of order, materials ordered and delivered from supplier, item manufactured, item delivered to customer, lapse of credit period, and finally cheques received from customers. Various types of business will have different trading cycles. For example, a retailer will not have a long period waiting for payment after the goods have been sold, but will have periods when large stocks of goods are on display or in warehouse awaiting sale. However, a common feature of most businesses is that they have to pay out cash for operational expenses before cash is received back from customers. Those outwards payments may be for all of the costs of sales (namely wages, materials and overheads) or merely for a proportion of them. The finance required to bridge the gap between those operational expenses payments and receipts of cash from customers is known as working capital.

A few moments thought about working capital should indicate that finance is not required for every transaction because in an on-going situation cash receipts from earlier transactions can be used to finance the operational expenses of later transactions, and provided the initial transactions can be financed by borrowed money, the later transactions can be self-financed by the business, – that is, later transactions are said to be 'internally financed'; but working-capital requirements will increase every time the volume of trading operations increases.

We can thus summarise the reason for the raising of finance by business as:

(1) a temporary imbalance between cash receipts and payments;
(2) the purchase of long-term assets; and
(3) working capital.

Table 2.1 illustrates the sources of finance to industrial and commercial companies in the United Kingdom in recent years, that is, the table illustrates the way in which those companies needs for finances were satisfied. The meaning of various selected items in Table 2.1 briefly is as follows:

Undistributed income – profit earned and retained within businesses. The profit has been calculated before allowing for depreciation of fixed assets, or appreciation to stock.

Bank borrowing – Basically overdrafts and other short-term bank finance.

Ordinary shares – the money raised by companies from the issue of *risk* capital on which shareholders may receive a dividend.

Debentures and preference shares – the money raised by companies issuing further long-term fixed-interest capital, that is, capital on which a fixed percentage *return* is paid each year. The interest or dividends on this type of capital would have a priority claim to profits before dividends on ordinary shares.

Capital transfers – this represents money received from government sources under its various schemes for transferring capital within the

Table 2.1

Sources of capital funds of industrial and commercial companies in the United Kingdom (£m.)

	Total	Undistributed income	Bank borrowing	Issues of securities (net)		Capital transfers	Other loans and mortgages	Overseas
				Ordinary shares	Debentures and preference shares			
1966	3837	2651	187	124	451	26	106	292
1967	4054	2684	333	65	350	236	28	358
1968	5472	3277	569	299	183	454	121	569
1969	5793	3223	664	177	335	598	211	585
1970	5888	3002	1125	39	154	526	306	736
1971	6388	3452	730	152	215	595	288	956
1972	9606	4571	2988	317	289	407	141	893
1973	13624	6229	4504	98	51	378	881	1483

Source: *Barclays Review* (August 1974); based on *Financial Statistics*.

economy. Examples would include regional development grants towards the cost of new equipment and buildings, and selective financial assistance granted under the Industry Act of 1972 for the relief of unemployment in certain areas.

Other loans and mortgages – this comprises hire-purchase debt, loans from the public sector and loans by financial institutions.

Overseas – this represents import and export credit, capital issues overseas and investment by overseas companies.

It is worth examining changes in the significance of the various sources of finance to industry and commerce over the period covered by Table 2.1.

A very significant feature of Table 2.1 is the importance of self-financing to companies via the medium of undistributed income/profit; but note how it has fallen in relative importance from 69 per cent in 1966 to 46 per cent in 1973. This of course means that an increased proportion of those companies' financial requirements has had to be found from external sources, the capital market. The most noticeable increase in those external sources has been in bank borrowings, which have risen from less than 5 per cent of sources in Table 2.1 in 1966 to 33 per cent in 1973. One must note that the proportion supplied by bank borrowing in 1973 was much higher than hitherto, but the 1970s generally have shown higher proportions than the 1960s.

Other loans and mortgages are shown in a thoroughly exceptional position in 1973 and probably reflect ingenuity at covering the void left by an inactive new issue market for shares and debentures. The rise and fall of capital transfers is likely to be associated with changing government politics, and overseas related finance has fluctuated over the period from about 8 per cent to nearly 11 per cent of the total, having reached as high as 15 per cent in 1971.

Perhaps the most striking feature of Table 2.1 is that it indicates the relatively small proportion of total funds supplied during those years by new issues of shares and debentures. (1974 and 1975 provided examples of extreme oscillation in the amounts raised by new share issues, and in fact 1975 was a record year.) It may occur to many readers that newspaper coverage of share activities as compared with banking gives no indication of their relative importance to business in the last decade. However, we will learn later that there have been huge sums of government stocks issued, and the cumulative total of previous issues of company securities is very substantial.

Table 2.1a

Summary of capital employed by 849 manufacturing and distribution companies at end 1974 (£m.)

Ordinary shares	5933
Preference shares	409
Capital and revenue reserves	13142
Long-term loans	5540
Bank overdrafts and short-term loans	6432
Deferred taxation and minority interests	3734
	35190

Source: *Financial Statistics.*

Table 2.1 showed the amounts of finance raised annually by industrial and commercial companies, and Table 2.1a shows the total amounts outstanding under some of those heads. Comparisons between the two tables are not particularly meaningful because of the different statistical populations and methods of preparation; but both are included for completeness.

Table 2.2 is particularly interesting as it reveals the proportions in which finance was recently supplied to enterprises in various countries. Certain incompatibilities between Tables 2.1 and 2.2 in respect of the United Kingdom can be explained by the different population of enterprises involved. It should be remembered that international comparisons are fraught with problems of differences in basic data in the countries of origin, and the most diligent efforts by compilers of such comparisons will probably still leave some residual problems.

It will be seen from the table that Japan uses borrowed capital much more than the other countries, and the United States provided a significantly larger proportion of its financial requirements internally than any of the others. This difference in approach to the financing of business is perhaps unexpected as both economies are so strong. It probably is due in part to the more established nature of U.S. industry, and the fast growth in Japanese industry not being sustainable without vast help from various financial institutions.

Another surprising feature to be revealed by Table 2.2 is that French and Italian companies, with their generally accepted less

Table 2.2

Sources of finance of enterprises (excluding financial institutions) in 1972* in percentage terms

	West Germany	United States	France	Italy	United Kingdom	Japan
GROSS SAVINGS	41·7	55·9	n.a.	33·9	41·7	34·5
CAPITAL TRANSFER (NET)	11·0	n.a.	n.a.	4·7	5·4	—
TOTAL BORROWING AND OTHER SOURCES	47·3	44·1	n.a.	56·2	52·9	65·5
of which in percentage terms						
Money market paper and short-term securities	0·6	−0·6	—	—	3·7	—
Short-term (including bank) loans	20·7	25·4	33·6	34·9	60·7	63·2‡
Shares	2·9	13·0	9·6	18·5	6·7	4·8
Bonds	3·2	15·3	15·4	8·2	5·6	1·3
Long-term bank loans	49·4 }	34·2 }	34·7 }	38·4† }	22·4 }	§
Other long-term loans	11·9	17·9	5·6		1·5	28·9
Trade credit	—			—		
Other	11·4	−5·3	1·0	—	—	1·8
STATISTICAL ADJUSTMENT	—	—	—	5·2	—	—

n.a. not available.
* France: 1971.
† Including medium-term loans.
‡ Including medium and long-term loans.
§ Included with short-term loans.
Sources: O.E.C.D., *Financial Statistics*, *Bank of Italy Annual Report*

well-developed capital markets, can finance a greater proportion of
their borrowed funds from share and bond issues than U.K.
companies, and note 1972 was a good year for the United Kingdom
in this respect (see Table 2.1). The latter is generally acknowledged
to possess one of the most sophisticated capital markets in the world,
whereas the French, for example, have a financial system which
relies much less on the 'market', and they have much greater state
direction of funds to borrowers. There is complementary evidence
mentioned in Table 2.3 below to suggest that U.K. industry is not
outstandingly well served with finance from the issue of new shares
and bonds.

Table 2.3

Issue of shares and bonds as a percentage of gross investment

	1969	1970
United States	24	42
Japan	14	14
West Germany	12	10
United Kingdom	9·5	8
France	7	9

Source: Peter Readman, The European Money Puzzle (London: Michael
Joseph, 1973). Readman's source is the *Commission des Operations de Bourse.*

There is much talk of U.K. industry not being as well equipped as
some of its competitors. Some would claim that this is because top
British management, for various reasons, has been reluctant to
spend the large sums on capital expenditure necessary to have a
modern industry. Certainly we mentioned earlier that Japan has
recently spent a greater proportion of its G.D.P. on capital formation.
We could perhaps use Table 2.4 to provide some support for the
comments that industry in the United Kingdom is having to use
outdated equipment. (Once again we offer a warning about problems
of comparing statistics internationally.)

It has also been said that there are substantial reasons for that
lack of expenditure on capital equipment. A common suggestion has
been that it is unlikely that a more extensive investment would have
proved sufficiently profitable because of poor management–worker
relations, and less co-operation by representatives of the latter than
is said to be the case in West Germany and Japan. However, for

Table 2.4

Manufacturing industry – investment per worker 1963–72 (£ per head, current prices)

	United Kingdom	United States	Japan	France	West Germany	Italy	Netherlands	Luxembourg	Belgium	Denmark	Eire
1963	122	330	183	283	214	184	229	—	222	217	159
1964	138	385	202	304	230	156	283	—	229	253	162
1965	153	444	163	318	256	131	298	—	261	284	198
1966	166	503	191	346	257	150	347	—	307	273	204
1967	167	534	288	372	247	173	376	—	321	297	211
1968	181	599	402	440	278	221	445	—	339	271	264
1969	209	652	502	497	372	251	474	—	386	347	320
1970	239	687	555	569	490	308	623	—	484	—	358
1971	272	713	513	623	521	339	675	—	508	—	—
1972	273	759	599	—	537	364	703	—	—	—	—

Source: *Trade and Industry* (21 November 1974).

further examination of these claims and counter-claims we must recommend readers to specialist books.

Table 2.4 was produced in answer to a parliamentary question and the reply was accompanied by the following warning: 'The information is given in the following table but the figures should not be used for any precise comparisons because of all the differences in coverage and definition.' Notwithstanding the honourable gentleman's comments, it does seem that an unfavourable picture of this aspect of U.K. industry is suggested.'

When discussing financial transactions involving individuals in the opening pages of this chapter, we mentioned two of the financial institutions commonly involved. Those institutions were banks and building societies. An early fact one learns when examining the financial institutions' involvement in the business sector is that building societies make virtually no loans to help finance the purchase of industrial and commercial premises. Nevertheless there are many financial institutions of other kinds actively involved in the process of transferring savings and other funds to business.

The clearing banks are very active in many guises. Their traditional function has been to lend short term to business (and others). Self-liquidating loans have been particularly favoured: for example, those of the type necessary to convert a purchase to a sale; but very often their short-term lending is renewed, rolled over, to a following period. In more recent years, banks have felt able to lend for longer periods because they themselves have been accepting deposits for longer periods. The clearing banks own a very large proportion of the hire-purchase sector, and also sometimes act in concert to set up specialist financial corporations like the Industrial and Commercial Finance Corporation (now part of Finance for Industry) – an organisation supplying long-term capital to small to medium-sized companies.

Much of the new issue of shares, debenture and loan capital is bought by insurance companies and pension funds with their accumulations of contributions to life assurance and superannuation schemes. Those contributions flow in steadily under long-term contracts, and in times when there is a dearth of new issues of securities by companies (as in 1973 and 1974) the insurance companies and pension funds could be faced with some investment problems.

Businesses often come into contact with government departments or government-sponsored agencies, which although acting in a way akin to the functions of financial institutions usually lend money or guarantee loans provided by others for specialist reasons. Those reasons include stimulating the purchase of new equipment, reducing unemployment, the development of new processes and ideas, and the furtherance of exports.

Borrowings by Public Corporations

The bulk of the public corporations are the nationalised industries, which at one time existed as privately owned big businesses, and subsequently were taken into public ownership. Most of the discussion in this section relates to nationalised industries. These organisations, like the businesses considered in the previous section, have to borrow money for working capital, because of a temporary mismatch between receipts and payments, and for the finance of capital expenditure for modernisation and expansion to the extent that such cannot be financed from internal cash flow.

The big difference in the supply of finance to the nationalised industries is that they have no direct access to the new issue section of the capital market. They do not now directly issue shares or debentures to the public, although soon after nationalisation some of them *did* issue loan stock. Nowadays when nationalised industries require external finance for capital expenditure, such money is usually first provided as it is incurred, by the banks as an overdraft, and subsequently that overdraft is repaid by a loan or grant received from central government. The transactions by central government to raise such funds to pay to private business, nationalised industries and local authorities are described towards the end of the chapter.

Nationalised industries also make use of the financial institutions in that they sometimes buy on hire purchase and lease equipment bought, for example, by insurance companies. Nationalised industries are also large borrowers of foreign funds, and a further source of finance to them is loans from their own pension funds.

Table 2.5 summarises the capital accounts of public corporations for certain recent years. It will be recalled from Table 2.1 that in the case of industrial and commercial companies, finance provided by undistributed income had fallen as a proportion of the whole over the period 1966–73. Table 2.5 indicates for public corporations that undistributed income has maintained its proportion of total funds required on capital account.

Table 2.5

Capital accounts of public corporations (£m.)

	1966	1970	1973	1974
Receipts				
Undistributed income before providing for depreciation and stock appreciation	653	831	1192	1317
Capital transfers (net)	11	331	695	223
Loans from central government (net)	843	605	138	699
Others	36	49	263	1023
	1543	1816	2288	3262
Expenditure				
Gross domestic fixed capital formation	1457	1679	2041	2692
Others	86	137	247	570
	1543	1816	2288	3262
Proportion of total provided by undistributed income (per cent)	43	45	52	40

Source: *National Income and Expenditure 1964–74.*

It has been suggested that the ability of a nationalised industry to bypass the scrutiny of the capital market when recourse to external finance is necessary removes one of the incentives to efficient management. What happens then is that the government's credit rating is substituted for that of an individual nationalised organisation, and therefore there is no spur to the management of the latter to achieve and maintain a good individual credit rating. Indeed, it has been suggested by some authorities that companies in the *private sector* should be encouraged to pay out more dividends and retain less profit so that shareholders could redirect their dividends to the companies likely to make the most efficient use of them. Companies would then have a reduced quantity of easily obtained finance, and would have to have performed well to attract some of the dividends reinvested by shareholders.

Any attempt to evaluate whether the performance of nationalised industries would benefit from having to compete for funds in the market is beset with problems. A very major problem would arise if such organisations were expected to compete in a *capital* market where performance was measured by profitability, but at the same time they were required to operate in a *trading* market where prices and the range of services offered were subject to ministerial and government influence. The latter could in turn be determined by national consumer interest, political opportunism and economic policy – for example to counter inflation.

It is sometimes thought that the capital market in practice does not sufficiently influence private-sector management towards greater efficiency and that top management's main motivation is towards security and enlargement of its own rewards. Such targets are likely to be best achieved by enlarging their business to a bigger organisation with bigger and better paid jobs.[2] Of course, expansion requires finance, as we have seen earlier, and it would seem illogical to imagine that the wishes of providers of finance can be ignored. Furthermore, if expansion is achieved by ploughing back profit, such profits have to be achieved in the first instance. Thus, although an important management goal may be expansion, this may only be achieved by pursuance of the shareholder's goal of maximising profit over the long term.

At this stage it will be informative to examine the balance sheets of a selection of nationalised industries, one each from transport, power, steel and communication, and to compare them with private-sector companies where appropriate. We have already mentioned that nationalised industries do not issue shares or debentures directly to the public, and it becomes very apparent from Table 2.6 that the government is the prime supplier of finance.

Government advances are the main source of finance and are usually provided on terms which require repayment in half-yearly instalments. The repayment period is long-term and ten to twenty years would be common, the interest rate payable is fixed from the outset and interest calculated on the balance outstanding. Some government finance is loaned for very short periods and is termed a 'bridging loan'. This could be used to finance the kind of temporary mismatch between receipts and payments which was mentioned earlier, whereas the longer-term loans would contribute to payment for capital expenditure and any required expansion of working capital.

An innovation in the kind of capital provided by government is public dividend capital, a form of capital on which a dividend is set by the relevant minister and which varies with the size of profits earned by the industry concerned.

The stocks mentioned in Table 2.6 are examples of issues by corporations in their early days and could be stock issued either as compensation for nationalisation or for capital expenditure/working capital in the early post-nationalisation years.

Table 2.6

*Financial structure of selected nationalised industries
end 1973–4 (£m.)*

	British Airways	British Gas	British Steel	Post Office
Stock	—	214	—	—
Public dividend capital	136	—	500	—
Government advances	116	1583	499	3019
Reserves	100	59	273	1031
Foreign loans	103	222*	45*	224*
Other loans	1	5	10	—
Minority interests	1	—	12	—
Regional development grants	—	—	149	—
Deferred liabilities	66	—	—	—
Bank loans and overdrafts	5	35	103	58
	528	2118	1591	4332
Extent of foreign finance (per cent)	20	11	3	5

* The greater part of this foreign capital was received in the latest accounting year.

Foreign loans represent a varying proportion of capital used by the nationalised industries, but even a quick glance at Table 2.6 shows that *British* gas is over 10 per cent financed by *foreign* loans (substantially in Deutsche marks and Swiss francs). British Steel has been helped out by the E.E.C. in the form of the European Investment Bank (E.I.B.) and by a U.S. dollar loan. The loan by the E.I.B. was a truly cosmopolitan affair and was made in a mixture of Belgian francs, Dutch florins and U.S. dollars. Loans are taken in foreign currencies for several reasons, and high on the list is the lower interest rates ruling overseas than in the United Kingdom. For example, the foreign loans received by British Steel in its 1973–4 accounting year were at 8½ per cent and 8⅝ per cent, whereas the additional loan received from the British government in the same period attracted interest at 11⅜ per cent. The foreign loans to British nationalised industries would attract guarantees by the British government as to payment of interest, principal and fluctuations in exchange rates. (The decline in the international value of sterling since these foreign currency loans were raised must cast some doubt on their over-all cheapness.) A second reason for accepting foreign currency loans is that such an inflow of currency goes some way to financing the U.K. balance-of-payments deficit, and might be encouraged because of that. It is also noticeable that the proportion of finance increased sharply in 1973–4.

'Minority interests' means that some proportion of the assets appearing in, for example, British Steel's balance sheet are owned by other people or organisations, but those organisations in total own less than 50 per cent of any of those assets.

Regional development and other grants include grants towards the cost of new buildings and equipment in geographical areas qualifying for financial assistance. The rates of grant vary from time to time and from sub-area to sub-area, and those grants have their roots in the post-1945 attempt to relieve regional unemployment in the United Kingdom. Steel plant, for example, would usually be situated in such areas. This supplement is often based on what is required to replace fixed assets at current price levels, and these of course, are, much higher than the original cost of such assets.

Reserves constitute surpluses of one kind or another which have been retained in the industries and used for modernisation and expansion. Such surpluses could have arisen on trading or on sales or revaluation of assets. There are substantial amounts included here representing supplementary charges for depreciation over and above the charge based on historical cost.

Bank loans and overdrafts are amounts borrowed ostensibly for short periods (up to six months) but which in practice tend to become of rather longer duration as the facility is renewed and rolled over from one period to the next. In time such short-term finance becomes funded, that is, turned into long-term money given permanence by being converted with a loan from the government.

Let us now examine how financial control is exercised over the activities of the nationalised industries and compare this with the principles applied in private-sector business. Both types of organisation will delegate areas of responsibility to various levels of management, and the performance of lower levels will be monitored by higher levels. Such monitoring and ensuing control usually involves a system of setting targets and reporting performance towards them, the targets often being embodied in a wider budgetary control system. What we would like to concentrate on here is the financial control exercised on top management. In various parts of this book we refer to the influence which is imposed from outside on top management of private-sector companies. Those influences include shareholders, statutory regulations – including regulations to make public certain matters such as operating results and individual costs, those with control over the supply of finance, and those outsiders with the ability to change top management.

Each nationalised industry has to observe the regulations of its controlling Act, and of course any general legislation which affects it, and the directions of its controlling minister. Parliament, the relevant minister and his civil servants exercise shareholder-type powers on their relationship with nationalised industries. The minister appoints board members and their chairman, agrees to capital-expenditure programmes, and, together with the Treasury, controls the means of raising the finance to pay for the plant, buildings and equipment in capital-expenditure programmes. Each of those industries has an over-all maximum limit set on its borrowing powers, and this is included in its controlling Act or amendments thereto. Such limits cover likely capital expenditure for several years ahead.

Private-sector companies for their part have borrowing powers limited by clauses in their Articles of Association, and the upgrading of these limits must be sanctioned by shareholders. However, private-sector companies do not usually have to seek approval for capital-expenditure programmes from a source outside its top management. There is the requirement for shareholders to accept the accounts and report of directors but they would not become involved with the strategy or detail inherent in the approval of capital-expenditure programmes *per se*. However, if additional finance were required from the shareholders or institutions, then they have broad control in the sense that the future prospects of the company must appear reasonably rosy or the supply of finance will not be forthcoming.

It seems that we have located the first of a number of steps in the financial control procedures of nationalised industries which are additional to the procedures for private-sector companies. Other differences include the formal publication of financial objectives and a public scrutiny of the comparison between actual performance and the objective. The non-nationalised companies only very exceptionally disclose their financial objectives, and it could be argued that they also therefore avoid any criticism should the target not be achieved. However, in defence of themselves, directors of private-sector companies would argue that they set themselves financial objectives in much the same form as the majority of nationalised industry targets are set. They fix a required percentage of earnings relative to the amount of capital employed in achieving those earnings. Private-sector management is also likely to argue that their targets, although unpublished, are higher than the nationalised industry targets and their achievement, whilst not being compared with an unpublished internal target, will be compared with the performance of their competitors. Such comparisons will be made by many, and financial journalists will ensure that they are published as prominently as possible. Furthermore, the degree of success they achieve, and are thought likely to achieve, is reflected in the relative movements of their share prices.

Turning back to the public sector there is also a further element in the financial overviewing of the nationalised industries in the form of the Select Committee on Nationalised Industries. This committee of the House of Commons is empowered

> to examine the Reports and Accounts of the Nationalised Industries established by Statute whose controlling Boards are appointed by Ministers of the Crown and whose annual receipts are not wholly or mainly derived from moneys provided by Parliament or advanced from the Exchequer.[3]

The Select Committee's method has been to take one industry at a time and to examine its reports over a number of years. In this way, it expects to examine each industry every six or seven years.

Borrowings by Local Authorities

Before we begin to look at how local authority activities are financed, let us first summarise the nature of those activities. We all have a fairly good idea that these are the supply of goods and services, particularly services, which are provided and administered locally. Visions of town halls and libraries, swimming pools and meals on wheels come readily to mind. From the outset it is convenient to draw a distinction between the provision of services and the provision of buildings, etc. within which the service is carried out, because the supply of finance is broadly split over those two areas. The type of finance attributable to those two parts has many differences, and the expenditure of those two types of finance is described as expenditure on current account and on capital account respectively. Current-account activities correspond to the trading activities of companies and nationalised industries, and capital-account expenditure is very similar to the capital expenditure of those organisations. Capital expenditure can usefully be described as the provision of a facility the use of which extends over a long period, certainly greater than a year and often much longer.

Local authorities have some current-account activities which generate income, for example housing and transport, but unlike companies and nationalised industries the local authorities have to look to local taxes (rates) and central government grants to pay for the greater part of the services they provide. Table 2.7 summarises local authorities' current-account expenditure and its finance for recent years.

Probably the most interesting observation concerning the finance of local authority current expenditure is the proportion paid for by central government grants and how that proportion has increased over the period 1966–74 from 46 per cent of such expenditure to 52 per cent thereof.

The local authorities also spend large sums on capital account (capital expenditure) providing new school buildings, school-meal cooking facilities, new roads and lights, and so on. Remember that Table 2.7 deals with the annual upkeep and operating costs of such services, whereas Table 2.8 explains how much money local authorities have spent on capital expenditure providing the facilities and its distribution over various headings. The second part of the table gives some details of the supply of finance for that expenditure, and we can immediately note that the first source is the annual surplus of current-account income over current-account expenditure of the local authorities.

The picture revealed by Table 2.8 is that for capital-expenditure purposes, local authorities borrowed £958 million in 1966 (546 + 412) and by 1974 the annual borrowing had risen to £3340 million (most of that increase arose in 1973 and 1974). Over the period 1966–74 approximately one-half of the total borrowings were supplied by central government and the other half from other sources.

Table 2.7

Local authorities' current expenditure and income (£m.)

	1966	1970	1973	1974
Current expenditure				
Education	1175	1777	2756	3393
Other social services (National Health Service, personal social services, school meals and milk)	322	500	830	927
Roads and public lighting	208	254	364	404
Sewerage and refuse	155	253	395	310
Police, fire and administration of justice	295	478	695	846
Other goods and services	223	334	514	672
Subsidies	86	116	137	178
Grants to personal sector	106	162	390	470
Debt interest	600	1068	1440	1878
General administration	75	90	146	211
	3245	5032	7667	9289
Current-account income				
Central government grants	1481	2450	4088	4819
Rates	1374	1824	2617	2991
Gross trading surplus	91	116	130	90
Rent	602	1006	1430	1678
Interest, etc.	84	109	179	347
	3632	5505	8444	9925
Surplus on current account	387	473	777	636

Source: *National Income and Expenditure 1964–1974.*

It is also worth noting that total current and capital expenditure by local authorities (local government) was financed to the extent of about 50 per cent by central government. We will examine in the next section the sources of central government finance, and merely comment at this point that it has to be substantial in view of the considerable sums also made available to the nationalised industries to finance their capital expenditure (Table 2.5, p. 32) and to industrial and commercial companies by various means.

The capital loans made available to local authorities by central government are nearly all received via the Public Works Loans Board (P.W.L.B.). The P.W.L.B. is prepared to lend up to 40 per cent of long-term borrowing by authorities, and even up to 50 per

Table 2.8

Local authorities' capital account expenditure and income (£m.)

	1966	1970	1973	1974
Capital expenditure				
Gross domestic fixed capital formation on:				
Education	185	295	467	481
Other social services	30	43	91	93
Roads and public lighting	112	246	333	347
Sewerage and refuse	83	158	281	140
Water	61	86	140	42
Police and fire	26	31	39	57
Housing	655	742	973	1649
Trading services	70	76	116	83
Capital sector grants mainly to personal sector	20	30	163	250
Net lending, mainly for house purchase	54	76	329	484
Others	123	174	325	388
	1419	1957	3257	4014
Capital receipts				
Surplus on current account	387	473	777	636
Central government grants	82	156	240	256
Loans from central government	546	722	1020	1265
Other identified borrowings	412	527	1345	2075
Others	−8	79	−125	−218
	1419	1957	3257	4014

Source: *National Income and Expenditure 1964–1974.*

cent for those authorities in less prosperous areas because they may have difficulties raising their capital requirements in the market. The loan period is related to the likely life of the assets and is made at rates close to those at which the central government can borrow.

Of the sources of finance used by local government other than central government, the banking sector has provided the greater part in recent years, but overdraft facilities do not feature very prominently. Such facilities are mainly used to cover very short-term needs and provide a buffer. Other financial institutions, for example life assurance companies, have supplied solid financial support for the local authorities, and during the five years 1969–73 the overseas sector provided nearly 10 per cent of those authorities' net borrowing. It is rather unexpected to learn that the banking sector is a large provider of funds to finance local authorities' *capital* expenditure (you will recall their current expenditure is more than adequately covered by current receipts – see Table 2.7). Banks normally lend the majority of their money for short periods, and one would expect capital expenditure to be financed with long-term money (money borrowed for long periods). However, the local authorities have financed much of their capital expenditure in recent years using short-term money (a significant proportion being bank money). This has been of some concern and central government has attempted to control this by various means, including a request that local authorities restrict their temporary borrowing to 20 per cent of their total borrowing, and the proportion for less than three months to 15 per cent of the total.

The bigger local authorities make public issues of long-term loans under the control of the Bank of England and these are quoted on the stock exchange.

An example of a recent local authority public issue is illustrated overleaf in an excerpt from an advertisement (from an issue of *The Times*) for a new issue of Greater London Loan Stock. The relevance of the yield and issue price should be clear following reading of Chapter 1, and attention is drawn to the purpose of the issue noted in the advertisement.

Shorter-term finance known as 'negotiable bonds', generally with a one-year life, may also be publicly issued and quoted, or they may be sold direct to discount houses. Local authorities have also raised considerable amounts for two to five year periods in the form of mortgages and bonds. Much of this money is provided in small sums in response to advertisements in the national and local press. Larger amounts can be provided in this form, and if so are raised from the institutions via the services of specialist brokers.

The scope of this book is to examine the nature and significance of the capital market. In order to put the capital-market operations of local authorities (and central government) into a financial perspective, we have described the wider environment into which the capital-market operations are slotted. We do not intend to comment in any detail on the rights and wrongs, efficiencies and deficiencies of the various methods used to raise local and central government *taxes*. We will just mention that the rating system of raising taxation has many critics who tend to be more vociferous and active than

THE LIST OF APPLICATIONS WILL BE OPENED AT 10.00 A.M. ON THURSDAY,
10th APRIL 1975 AND WILL BE CLOSED ON THE SAME DAY

GREATER LONDON COUNCIL

GREATER LONDON
12½ per cent STOCK, 1982

ISSUE OF £75,000,000 AT £97.75

PAYABLE AS FOLLOWS:

On application	£10.00 per cent
On Thursday, 8th May, 1975	£30.00 per cent
On Monday, 23rd June, 1975	£57.75 per cent
	£97.75 per cent

INTEREST PAYABLE HALF-YEARLY ON 25th MAY
AND 25th NOVEMBER

The issue is made in accordance with a General Consent given by the Treasury under the Control of Borrowing Order 1958. The Stock is an investment falling within Part II of the First Schedule to the Trustee Investments Act 1961. Application has been made to the Council of The Stock Exchange for the Stock to be admitted to the Official List.

The Stock is created by a Resolution of the Greater London Council dated 3rd October 1972, and is issued pursuant to the provisions of the Local Government Act 1972. THE GOVERNOR AND COMPANY OF THE BANK OF ENGLAND are authorised to receive applications for the Stock.

1 PURPOSE OF ISSUE

The proceeds of the issue will be used to replace monies borrowed temporarily to meet capital expenditure pending the raising of loans; to redeem other loans falling due for repayment; to finance further capital expenditure of the Council as authorised by the Council's annual Money Acts; to make advances to bodies and persons to whom the Council is authorised to lend money; and for other purposes for which the Council is authorised to borrow.

critics of central taxes. Perhaps because of the local nature of the burden, members of a community think they can organise pressure more easily and have greater effective criticism of alleged local overspending than they can hope to have when critical of central government extravagance.

The nature of local government finance is being investigated currently by the Layfield committee and it has a most difficult task.

Two suggestions made to the Layfield committee include a local income tax collected centrally through the inland revenue but at a rate determined by the local authorities, and a local petrol tax as a supplement to the national fuel tax.[4]

Finally, in this section on local authorities we summarise in Table 2.9 the amounts owing by local authorities and the form in which it is owed.

Table 2.9

Outstanding local authority longer-term debt, 1973–5 (£m.)

Quoted securities	1764
Negotiable bonds	667
P.W.L.B. mortgages	8255
Other long-term debt	5900
Total	16586*

* Note that the totals for 1974 and 1975 were £18,375 m. and £20,548 m. respectively.
Source: *Financial Statistics.*

Borrowings by Central Government

We have already encountered the role of central government as a supplier of finance to privately owned business, for example regional development grants and selective financial assistance for the reduction of unemployment; to nationalised industries, for example to finance their new capital expenditure programmes; and to local authorities to finance about half of their current expenditure and some of their capital expenditure. We would also expect central government to have some very large expenditure on other services it supplies. Fairly obvious examples of such services are defence costs, national insurance and health, and education not administered by local government; there are many other examples as well.

The bulk of central government's annual spending is a charge on what is known as the 'consolidated fund', and such expenditure is financed in the main by some form of taxation. The events of 1973–5 are provided in a very summarised form in Table 2.10.

We note that central government is 'short of money' and needs to raise further finance, perhaps by a loan. But that is not the end of their extra financing requirements, and we can see from Table 2.11, the 'national loans fund', that government had a requirement of a further £1403 million to finance its loans to local authorities, etc. for their capital expenditure, and to refinance the paying back (redeeming) of previous loans to central government.

We have now located that in 1973–4 central government had an apparent borrowing requirement of £1739 million + £1403 million that is £3142 million, and by 1974–5 it had grown to £5583 million. (The trend since 1969–70, when there was a surplus of over £1000 million, has been one of reducing balances and later increasing

Table 2.10

Consolidated fund (£m.)

	1973–4	1974–5
Expenditure		
Supply services (including defence, local government social services, agriculture, trade and industry)	18624	25605*
Debt interest	677	576
Northern Ireland	350	421
E.E.C.	219	243
Others	95	−43
	19965	26802
Revenue		
Inland revenue (including income tax and corporation tax)	10633	14191*
Customs and excise	6220	7407*
Motor vehicle duties	533	532
Selective employment	45	2
Miscellaneous receipts	795	1438
	18226	23570
Deficit	1739	3232*

* These increases are particularly noteworthy.
Source: *Financial Statistics.*

Table 2.11

National loans fund (£m.)

	1973–4	1974–5
Loans to:		
Local authorities	1000	1130
Nationalised industries	174	578
Other public corporations including new towns and commissions	217	627
Private sector (net repayment)	−6	−7
Lending within central government	18	23
	1403	2351

Source: *Financial Statistics.*

borrowing requirements each year.) The way in which those requirements were provided is summarised in Table 2.12.

Table 2.12
Financing of government borrowing requirements (£m.)

	1973–4	1974–5
Issue to the public of British Government Securities	1651	2177
Net redemption/issue of Treasury bills	−347	1597
Others including overseas official financing	−243	951
Net indebtedness to the Bank of England	704	−544
Notes and coins	454*	921*
Surplus on national insurance funds (note this is not included in Table 2.10)	271	605
Departmental balances and miscellaneous	652	−124
	3142	5583

* Oh that a few more of us could print our own money to pay for our requirements!
Source: *Financial Statistics.*

The British Government Securities mentioned in Table 2.12 represent a huge call upon the savings of the nation and those securities would have been purchased by various institutions. Some of those securities were long dated (for example the issue of £573 million 12 per cent Treasury Loan would not be redeemed for ten years) and such securities would have been taken up traditionally by life assurance companies and various pension funds. It is also possible that many other institutions may have viewed alternative outlets for their savings and decided that those securities were a good buy. Another part of the over-all issue of British Government Securities in 1973–4 was £593 million 10½ per cent of Treasury Stock, to be redeemed in 1976. Such stock would have been attractive to those institutions wanting shorter-term investments and it is possible that the banking sector was tempted to subscribe to that issue.

Any part of an issue of British Government Securities which is not required by the public immediately is taken up by the Bank of England or National Debt Commissioners and subsequently sold to the public when there is a demand for it. Treasury bills are also mentioned in Table 2.12 and these are short-term loans to the government (ninety days) provided by the banks and discount market.

The sum of all such issues of Government Securities to the

public, since such issues began, which are still outstanding is collectively known as the National Debt. The National Debt is to some extent backed up by assets (derived from the capital expenditure of, for example, nationalised industries, and local government), and this part is known as 'reproductive debt'. But some securities were issued to finance warfare, for example British Government $3\frac{1}{2}$ per cent War Loan, and others were issues to finance the excess of government's current expenditure over its current revenue. By end-March 1975 the size of the National Debt was £44,495 million.

Summary

In this chapter we have provided a backcloth to those who are the fund-raisers in the United Kingdom, why they need to raise finance, the form of loan they raise and, broadly, who supplies the finance. We have omitted discussing individuals except for a brief entrée to other areas, and have noted how the central government's tentacles spread far into the realms of finance of all sectors.

We broadly followed a pattern which first looked at how much finance was raised by the various sectors each year, and we followed that by mentioning the different forms of that finance and its suppliers, and finally we disclosed how much was owed by each sector over all or by prominent members of it at a given date.

We would like to conclude by showing the distribution of capital formation on fixed assets over the various sectors for 1973 and 1974 (Table 2.13).

Table 2.13

Gross domestic fixed capital formation (£m.)

	1973	1974
Personal sector	2537	2309
Companies	5699	7020
Public corporations	2041*	2692*
Central government	773	946
Local authorities	2765†	3280†
	13815	16247

* As in Table 2.5.

† As in Table 2.8 less items relating to capital grants to the personal sector and lending for house purchase.

Source: *National Income and Expenditure 1964–1974.*

Further Reading

James Bellini, William Pfaff, Laurence Schloesing, Edmund Stillman with Michael Barth, *The United Kingdom in 1980: The Hudson Report* (London: Associated Business Programmes, 1974).

K. Midgley and R. G. Burns, *Business Finance and the Capital Market* (London: Macmillan, 1972) chs. 3, 5.

Anthony Sampson, *The New Anatomy of Britain* (London: Hodder & Stoughton, 1971). Ch. 35, 'Nationalised Industries'.

W. Thornhill, *The Nationalised Industries* (London: Nelson, 1968), particularly ch. 5, 'Finance'.

A. J. Whiteside, *General Financial Knowledge* (London: HFL (Publishers) Ltd, 1965) chs. viii–x.

Barclays Review (August 1974), various articles.

Midland Bank Review (August 1968) 'Financing the Nationalised Industries'.

The Chartered Institute of Public Finance & Accounting, evidence to the Committee of Inquiry into Local Government Finance, *Public Finance and Accountancy*, supplement (February 1975).

Central Statistical Office, *National Income and Expenditure 1964–1974* (London: H.M.S.O., 1975).

The *Annual Accounts* of the nationalised industries.

CHAPTER 3
Suppliers of Funds-
A Profile of Investors and
their Relative Influence

In this chapter we look at the supply side of the market for funds (that is, the buying side of the market for securities). An analysis of the type of lenders, the channels used by them, the degree of skill employed and the influence they exert are all matters which are relevant to this study of the capital market and the consideration of its effectiveness. The emphasis is on long-term investment by individuals and financial institutions, particularly in the company sector; in addition brief consideration is given to the activities of some specialist suppliers of finance.

The Personal Sector

Most adults in the United Kingdom are at least indirect investors – through their holdings of life assurance policies, their interest in superannuation funds, or their deposits in bank accounts. It would be useful to know exactly how capital is distributed amongst the different holders, but we shall have to be content with approximations. Statistics have tended to concentrate on income flows, although some fairly accurate figures on the ownership of ordinary shares have been compiled over recent years by J. Revell and J. Moyle of the Department of Applied Economics of Cambridge University.[1]

Estate duty estimates provide a starting point for the calculation of personal wealth holdings. Adjusted to a valuation at current market prices, the U.K. estimated figures for net wealth of the personal sector, as presented by the Diamond Commission on the Distribution of Income and Wealth, are as shown in Table 3.1 for end-1972. The figures are more useful as a means of indicating the different types of wealth holding than as an accurate comparison

Table 3.1

	(£m.)
Dwellings	65125
Land and other buildings	13339
Consumer durables	14195
Trade assets	5529
All physical assets	98188
Quoted government stocks	2740
Quoted company equities	24185
Unit trusts	2082
Overseas companies	1969
Unquoted U.K. government	4707
Other government securities	1416
Other U.K. company stocks	6314
Cash and bank deposits	11864
Savings bank deposits	4686
Other deposits	15671
Life policies	17563
Loans and debtors	12703
All financial assets	105900
All assets	204088
Less liabilities	30199
Net wealth	173889

Source: Royal Commission on the Distribution of Wealth, *Report No. 1*, Cmnd. 6171 (London: H.M.S.O. 1975) table 33.

of the values of the various holdings. These will of course vary in size from day to day and month to month with the fluctuations in the various markets. The pattern of such holdings, and changes in the pattern, nevertheless have a bearing on the behaviour of the capital market; for example, changes in preference for different forms of wealth have their effects on security values and interest rates. An increased liquidity preference will lower security prices and raise rates of return and vice versa. Similarly, if property is favoured in preference to securities, security prices and rates of return will be affected.[2]

This wealth is by no means evenly spread among the population, although the distribution pattern varies somewhat accordingly to the method of calculation. There is little doubt, however, that over the past sixty years there has been a steady movement towards a more even spread among the top 20 per cent of wealth owners, although there have been a less dramatic change in the ownership of the bottom 80 per cent of wealth holders (see Table 3.2).

Table 3.2

Wealth distribution among wealth holders for selected years

	Top 1%	Top 5%	Top 10%	Top 20%	Bottom 80%
1911–13	69	87	92	n.a.	n.a.
1936–8	56	79	88	n.a.	n.a.
1960	38	64	77	90	10
1965	33	58	73	89	11
1970	29	56	70	89	11
1974*	24	48	65	86	14

* Estimate.
Source: Royal Commission on the Distribution of Wealth, *Report Nos. 1 and 2*, Cmnd. 6171/2.

Further aspects of distribution of wealth are: there is a bias towards older people having greater wealth; men own more wealth than women (but women's share increased from 33 to 42 per cent between 1931 and 1960, although it has fallen slightly since then); when pension rights are brought into account, there is a greater levelling up; since 1960 land and dwellings have increased as a proportion of total assets and Stock Exchange securities have fallen; life assurance and building society assets have also grown relative to other assets.

With regard to equity holdings in quoted companies (which, although numbering a mere 3000 or so, control more assets, in terms of value, than the other 600,000 or so non-quoted companies), there has been a tendency for many years now for a steady reduction in the holdings of private investors. (This has continued during recent years in spite of an increase in personal saving as a percentage of total personal disposable income from 8 per cent in 1968 to 12 per cent by 1974 and the promise of an even higher level of saving in 1975.) The annual disinvestment in company shares by private investors has, however, been offset by increased investment in financial intermediaries such as insurance companies (via life policies, and so on) pension funds, investment trusts and unit trusts.[3] This changing pattern of equity holdings can be seen from Table 3.3.

Several reasons may be put forward for the continued decline in

Table 3.3

Ownership of quoted ordinary shares in U.K. companies (percentage)

	1963	1969	1973
Persons	58·7	47·0	42·0
Institutional investors			
Insurance companies (life)	10·6⎫	12·4⎫	14·2⎫
Pension funds	7·0⎪	9·4⎪	12·1⎪
Investment trusts	6·7⎬25·5	7·0⎬31·7	6·5⎬36·3
Unit trusts	1·2⎭	2·9⎭	3·4⎭
Charities,			
non-financial companies			
overseas holders etc.	15·7	21·3	21·7

If investment trust and other inter-company holdings are vetted out and redistributed to their ultimate owners, the pattern becomes as follows:

	1963	1969	1973
Persons	69·0	56·4	50·0
Institutional investors	20·9	29·7	35·6
Others	10·1	14·0	14·4

Source: J. Moyle, *The Pattern of Ordinary Share Ownership 1957–1970* (Cambridge University Press, 1971); and Royal Commission on the Distribution of Wealth, *Report No. 1*, Cmnd. 6172.

personal holdings of ordinary shares, perhaps the most important of these being the growing diversity of alternative outlets for savings. Unit trusts in particular provide a convenient alternative to direct shareholding for the small investor. They make it possible for such investors to place small amounts of savings in units and thus gain the advantage of a spread of equity investments and avoid some of the risk associated with single holdings or holdings in a very narrow range of securities. Since the first unit trust (First British Fixed Trust) was formed in 1931 there has been a steady increase in interest in this form of investment, and during the 1960s and early 1970s the expansion has been particularly rapid.

The other institutional investors have not expanded quite so quickly but in each case their equity holdings are considerably larger than those of the unit trusts. They too offer a stake in equities with rather less risk than that which direct investment incurs. Many employed persons have little choice about investing in equities through pension funds, and, moreover, this form of investment tends to rise in proportion to the rise in incomes. Since 1945, when equity holdings represented only 9 per cent of assurance company assets, the proportion of equity holdings has risen to about 25 per cent, so that with-profit endowment policy-holders are also indirect investors

in equities. Any form of investment through these financial intermediaries avoids the trouble and expense of maintaining a personal
portfolio of ordinary share holdings. Moreover, there may be
certain economies to be enjoyed by investing through intermediaries:
premiums payable to insurance companies are subject to certain
income tax relief; superannuation fund contributions similarly are
deductible for income tax purposes; the investment income of
pension funds is not taxable and insurance companies pay a reduced
rate; brokers' charges are relatively less for the large dealings of
institutional investors as compared with the small transactions of the
private investor; and finally, referring this time to investment trusts,
it is frequently possible for a private investor to purchase shares in an
investment trust at a discount on the value of the underlying equity
holdings of the trust.

Although the above comments help to explain why direct personal
investment has tended to decline in terms of percentage holdings
of equities available, the fact remains that private investors still
hold between 40 and 50 per cent of equities, according to the
method of measurement used, and it is not impossible that the
trend against direct investment may be reversed at some time in the
future if tax and market regulations become more favourable. In the
meantime many private investors must still be presumed to prefer
to back their own judgement and exercise some degree of control
over the distribution of their investments in different companies.
Their degree of control over the management of the companies in
which they invest is another matter, and this we shall consider
shortly.

The declining holdings of private shareholders in percentage
value terms does not imply that the actual number of private
investors is decreasing. Generally, persons represent over 90 per
cent of all holders of the shares of a large company. Of these,
between 70 and 90 per cent will typically be small shareholders
with holdings of less than £2000 in value. The number of small
shareholders is probably increasing, but the average size of their
holdings appears to be diminishing. An estimate by the British
Market Research Bureau Ltd on behalf of the London Stock
Exchange in 1965 suggested that about 1,800,000 people in the
United Kingdom held shares (although twenty-two million people
were indirect investors through life assurance and pension funds).[4]
A later survey, the 1971 Chesham Pilot Study,[5] suggested a trend

towards a wider spread of ownership. A figure of $2\frac{1}{2}$ million share-holders was estimated. Generally, there was a bias towards older, better-educated and professional people in the shareholder profile, although the later study suggested that a greater proportion of younger people were holding shares in 1971 than in 1965.

An issue which deserves some attention in this chapter is the degree of influence, direct and indirect, which these $2\frac{1}{2}$ million or so of private shareholders may exert. Do they, for example, acquire information concerning their companies promptly, or at least at the same time as other investors, and do they act on such information by selling their shares if the outlook for the company concerned has deteriorated, or buy on hearing good news of particular com-panies? One thing seems clear, and that is that the great majority of these private shareholders do not receive information concerning their companies as quickly as those investors (private or institu-tional) who are centred close to City events, partly because of inevitable postal delays but also partly because of the ready accessi-bility to special channels of information available to certain in-vestors.[6] In the latter case this may or may not involve access to 'inside information'. If the delays in receipt of information by the many 'outsiders' resulted in their dealing in the opposite manner to that which would have applied had the information been known, then the share price would not respond correctly to the information, thus inhibiting the operation of market forces as discussed in Chapter 1. However, it seems reasonable to assume that of those shareholders or potential investors who are ignorant of the true course of events, as many will act in one direction as those who act in the other; in other words the effect of ignorance will be self-cancelling.

A great deal of information is available to shareholders,[7] even if it is not received as promptly as many would wish. The most important, and usually the most up-to-date, source is that provided by the company itself, that is the annual report and accounts and also the interim statement. The former gives details, *inter alia*, of the profit or loss for the current and previous year, including disclosure of various items of expense, the assets and liabilities of the company, the directors of the company, and the chairman's assessment of the company's performance during the year in his report. Various registers give information concerning members of the company, debenture holders, directors and charges secured on the assets of the company, the Stock Exchange publishes a *Daily Official List* giving official quoted prices, a *Year Book*, a quarterly *Fact Book* and various other statistical items, but the small private shareholder is likely to be more influenced by *advice* rather than cold statistical facts. This he may obtain from the City columns of his newspaper, from specialist journals, such as the *Investors Chronicle*, or from a broker, either direct or via a bank manager.

There is then no shortage in quantity of information, although sophisticated investors may complain about the quality. As might be expected the average small investor does not pore over all the information at his disposal until he has trained himself to be a veritable wizard of finance. The 1965 *Stock Exchange Survey* revealed that although private shareholders are better informed on financial matters than the rest of the population generally, their knowledge was nevertheless much less than satisfactory. Only two-thirds of the shareholders participating knew what 'gilt-edged' meant; less than a third knew which type of share gave voting rights, only a third followed prices regularly, and 86 per cent had never been to a company meeting. In 1968 I.C.I. Ltd conducted a survey enquiring into the readership of the *Annual Report*. It was revealed that about three-quarters of the shareholders read the *Report* – on average four items in it, the sections summarising the trading results and finance being the most widely read. About 40 per cent of the participants expressed a preference for a shorter, summarised form of report and only 15 per cent wished to have more information.

As to the extent to which private shareholders react to such information as they do peruse, some further findings from the Chesham Study help to fill in the picture. Almost half the shareholders in this survey held shares in only one company, and only 18 per cent held shares in six companies or more. Almost half the shares held by participants in this study had been held for more than ten years. A quarter of the participants had never bought any shares, while over half had never sold any. Only one shareholder in six had bought shares during the six months previous to the study, and one in seven had sold during that time.

Clearly a high proportion of private shareholders are not active in the sense of buying or selling shares in response to new information which becomes available and to the changing pattern of economic and political events. This does not mean to say that there is not a large *number* of private shareholders who *are* active. It seems that there may be many thousands of private shareholders who are extremely active, and many more thousands who are moderately active, but of course these represent a fairly small proportion of the whole. In fact from a *One Day Transaction Study* for 7 August 1974 by the Stock Exchange the following points emerged: three-quarters of *all* bargains (that is, including fixed-interest stocks) and four out of every five bargains in British equity stocks were for private clients; and private individuals accounted for 31 per cent of bargains by *value* in British and Irish equities, while institutions were responsible for 53 per cent. (The balance was largely accounted for by overseas clients).

If this study were representative of transactions generally, it would seem that in spite of the larger number of their transactions over all, private shareholders were exerting less influence on the market than the institutions.

As we saw in Chapter 1 investors' behaviour in the market, via changing share prices, operates so as to provide incentives and penalties to company management. We shall now consider briefly whether private shareholders exert a more direct influence on company management in their capacity as ultimate controllers through the voting system (assuming that they hold voting shares and not shares with restricted voting rights).

Anyone who has attended company meetings and who is acquainted with a cross-section of small private shareholders might be forgiven for forming an opinion that such influence is negligible and that shareholders are apathetic. Certainly such a person would be aware that the number of shareholders attending meetings is very small: indeed generally well below 1 per cent of members attend and usually less than 20 per cent trouble to vote.[8] However, it is wrong to assume that private shareholders are disinterested in their investments; it is not a common facet of human nature to be unconcerned about the value and safety of possessions. On the other hand, small shareholders, though not apathetic, are almost certainly pragmatic about their role. Although many of them may make reasonable use of the annual report, most of them are neither sufficiently skilled nor sufficiently well-informed to make a useful direct contribution to the supervision of company management. A visit to London to attend an annual general meeting would cost the equivalent of their annual dividend in many instances, and although they can vote by post they are aware that either the issues are of a minor matter, or if they are, for example in the case of a company which is being badly managed, of major importance, that they are not sufficiently in touch with the centre of things to make a sensible contribution. Even those private shareholders who are skilled in the analysis of accounts and reports may find the effort and cost of attempting to gain the support of other shareholders, in order to put pressure on the management, too daunting to pursue. Nevertheless, it must be said that at least a few shareholders and private shareholders' associations have taken considerable pains to analyse information made available by their companies or extracted from them as a result of persistent questioning. Where not satisfied with the direction of their companies, they have persuaded other shareholders to use their proxy votes on behalf of their campaign and have, *inter alia*, defeated directors' proposals, resisted takeover recommendations, and/or elected their own nominees to the board.[9] Such persons and bodies have no doubt exercised influence out of all proportion to their numbers and the value of their holdings, but in many instances their efforts have failed because of lack of funds, insufficient support, inadequate information and, inevitably, strong counter-attacks from the board. It may indeed be the case that the legal structure of corporate control is unduly ponderous and that there is a need for properly elected *representatives* of shareholders to act on a permanent basis as a supervisory body. Institutional shareholders may already exert influence on company management through representative bodies, as will be explained in the section to follow. Furthermore, supporters of workers' participation in management are realistic enough to appreciate that if company policy is to be influenced, then the procedure to be adopted should involve *representation* at board level rather than any attempt to operate through a general employees' meeting. If private shareholders are to exert an effective form of direct control, then they too may aim for formal representation rather than rely on the largely sterile area of the formal meeting and voting procedures or on the disruptive, though not necessarily unproductive process of ginger-group activity.

Institutional Investors

Features which distinguish institutional investors are: (1) that they are intermediaries, that is they invest on behalf of others: (2) that they generally have much larger sums at their disposal for investment than individual shareholders; (3) there are comparatively few of them, and they can more easily act in concert; and (4) particularly in the case of insurance companies and pension funds, they tend to have a net inflow of funds available for investment. In the equity market one aspect of institutional operations is that as their percentage holdings of ordinary shares increase, the floating supply of these shares will diminish at a proportionately greater rate, thus amplifying the effect on prices of further purchases or sales by the institutions. The various other factors affecting the stock market at any time, such as the level of new issues, make it difficult to gauge this effect with any precision, but both U.K. and U.S. studies seem to indicate that institutional shareholders tend to trade *with* rather than *against* major cyclical price trends.[10]

Some measure of the influence on market prices by a particular group of investors may be taken by relating that group's trading activity to the total for the market. Perhaps somewhat surprisingly, in view of their steadily increasing share of total equity holdings, the equity turnover of the combined institutional investors has not diverged greatly from about 40 per cent of total equity turnover on the London Stock Exchange, as the figures in Table 3.4 reveal.

Table 3.4

Combined institutions' share of total equity turnover on the London Stock Exchange (percentage)

1966	1967	1968	1969	1970	1971	1972
40·1	39·4	41·7	45·0	45·3	40·6	42·5

Source: R. Dobbins and M. J. Greenwood, 'Institutional Shareholders and Equity Market Stability', *Journal of Business Finance and Accountancy*, vol. 2, no. 2 (Summer 1975) table 1.

(Annual figures of this sort do not of course mean that such averages are typical of daily trading and the *One Day Transaction Study* previously referred to showed that 53 per cent of bargains by value in British and Irish equities were accounted for by institutions.) Institutional investors have sometimes had attributed to them the function of stabilising market prices at times of accentuated price swings (resulting from the activities of other investors). Evidence of this, and, incidentally, evidence of superior dealing acumen, could take the form of institutional net acquisitions at the time of market troughs and net disposals at the time of market peaks.

However, an enquiry into correlation between the *Financial Times* All-Share Index and net acquisitions (a negative coefficient indicating 'stabilising activity' – low acquisitions at market peaks and vice versa) found that only investment and unit trusts could be considered to have any 'stabilising' influence.[11] This does not mean that *individual* institutional investors fail to operate profitably at peaks and troughs of general share prices. Nor does it mean that institutional investors generally fail to invest wisely at times other than peaks and troughs.

Insurance companies and superannuation funds not only differ from unit trusts and investment trusts in that they can be assured of a steady inflow of funds, but also in the size and variety of their holdings. Comparisons in terms of size cannot be very accurate because of different methods of valuation in published statistics and, particularly in recent years, because of widely fluctuating market prices of securities. The relative size of the four main types of institutional investor in terms of equity holdings was indicated earlier in this chapter, but whereas unit trusts and investment trusts invest much the greater part of the funds at their disposal in ordinary shares, pension funds and insurance companies hold a variety of other securities in addition to equities. A rough idea of these differences in holdings can be given if the different holdings are shown as percentages of total holdings, although, as previously pointed out, the percentage value of equity holdings can vary considerably according to the state of the equity market (see Table 3.5).

Although a large part of the assets of pension funds and insurance companies is invested outside the area of company shares and debentures, it must not be thought that such investments are alien to the capital market. Funds made available to companies as a result of a sale of property (and leaseback) or as a loan against property may be put to just as good use as funds generated by an issue of shares or debentures. Moreover, even the funds invested in government securities may be indirectly financing nationalised industries or financing private industry, for example in the form of investment grants to industries in the Development Areas.[12] In this part of the discussion, however, we are mainly concerned with the influence of institutional investors in the equity market, and we now turn briefly to the more direct influence which they may exert on company management.

Table 3.5

*Percentage holdings of different types of securities held by
institutional investors at end 1974**

	Insurance companies	Superannuation funds	Investment trusts	Unit trusts
Ordinary shares	21	43	73	67
Land, property and ground rents	16	14	—	—
Loans and mortgages	13	4	—	—
Company debentures	11	9	3	1
Government and local authority securities	23	16	3	2
Short-term assets	12	11	16	28
Other	4	3	5	2
Total investments (£m.)	24357	9414	3770	1405

* Insurance company investment percentages are based on book values;
the other institutions' investments on market values. The percentages are
approximations and are rounded to the nearest whole number. Note that
the short-term assets held by the trusts are unusually high at end 1974 after
a period of lost confidence in equities.
Source: *Financial Statistics.*

Some individual institutional investors are large enough to
command attention from company management without the need
to consort with fellow institutions. For example, the Prudential
Assurance Company controls ordinary shares which amount to
something approaching one-fifth of all insurance company equity
holdings, and thus has substantial voting rights in many of the
well-known large U.K. companies. In spite of this, even the larger
individual investors do participate with other investors to protect
their interests in the companies whose shares they hold. Thus
insurance companies may bring their combined weight to bear
through their British Insurance Association's Investment Protection
Committee, and investment trusts through the Association of
Investment Trusts, both bodies dating back to the early 1930s.
Pension funds and unit trusts also may operate through their own
associations, and, in order to co-ordinate the control activities

of individual institutions and their representative bodies, the Institutional Shareholders' Committee was formed in 1973 on the initiative of the Governor of the Bank of England.

The crux of the problem for institutional investors is that if they attempt to sell large holdings in companies which are badly managed, they may only create further losses for themselves, as, by unloading large quantities of shares on to the market, they will be driving the share price down against themselves. They thus have a strong motive to try to ensure that the companies in which they invest are efficiently managed. But self-interest is not the sole motivation; the institutions have also been sensitive to criticism by the press and other shareholders of their apparent lack of resolve in dealing with unsatisfactory company situations. The general tenor of the criticism has been that while the current legal provisions for control of companies leave little scope for supervision of their investments by the vast number of small and dispersed shareholders, the powerful institutions, concentrated mainly in the City of London and aided by expert investment analysts, that is bodies which could take action in appropriate cases, have frequently not wielded the power which lies in their hands.

Such criticism is not entirely fair on two counts: first, that, particularly in recent years, there have been many instances of successful interference in company affairs by institutions, though often behind the scenes, so that such incidents are not usually brought to the notice of the general public; second, that although it is an easy enough matter to interfere in a company's internal affairs, it is not easy to undertake such intervention successfully.

One of the problems facing influential shareholders who are dissatisfied with company performance is that of distinguishing between situations resulting from unsatisfactory management and those which stem from circumstances beyond management control. In the latter instances, although the institutions may be able to offer advice, they may be wise to avoid direct interference. Another problem is that their main expertise lies in the field of finance whereas the problems which face company management may range over such areas as labour relations, export promotion and technological difficulties in production. This latter obstacle can be overcome by engaging the services of experts in appropriate fields (for example management consultants) to advise on particular issues.

More positively, there are several ways in which institutions can contribute to management efficiency. Perhaps the most on-going contribution they can make is to analyse the accounts and other information of their investment companies and interrogate management on weaknesses which have been revealed. They may also require the appointment of a director or directors of their choice and/or insist on an adequate number of non-executive directors on the board. Other forms of supervision may include the insistence on the dismissal of a managing director or other directors, the right to be consulted on key issues such as takeover bids, rights issues, major changes of objectives and executives' incentive schemes.

Institutions may also use the weight of their funds to influence events, although the prime aim of such manoeuvrings may not necessarily be to promote company efficiency; for example, they may rig the market to enable a company to make a bid on more advantageous terms or engage in legitimate stock promotion to cause the share price of a certain company to rise and so improve the performance of the institutional fund.[13]

It may be thought that because the institutions hold well over a third of the shares of large companies, and also have large holdings in many of the smaller quoted companies, they hold the key to company efficiency. However, the institutions do not exercise continuous supervision, but rather begin to take a serious interest in control *after* signs of indisposition begin to appear. Investment managers who organise and co-ordinate the activities of institutional protection committees may not have the same personal incentive to intervene in company affairs as private investors. Thus, in spite of the apparent power wielded by institutional investors, there may be a need for their co-operation with representatives of private investors for the purpose of providing continuous supervision of individual companies.

Other Suppliers of Funds – Bank Finance

Much of the foregoing has been concerned with the supply of long-term funds, particularly those funds which have been directed into the equity market. While our emphasis is mainly on the longer end of the market for funds, it must be acknowledged that there is no hard and fast definition of the capital market which excludes medium- and shorter-term borrowing and lending of funds. Fund-raisers may often have a choice as to how they finance their capital projects, their final decision perhaps depending on economic conditions at the time. In the following brief review of other suppliers of funds the discussion is therefore not confined to long-term financing.

The most important source of supply of external funds outside the equity and debenture markets is bank lending. Until fairly recently bank loans and overdrafts were mainly available to meet the needs of industry and commerce for working capital; that is, most bank loans were of the self-liquidating type, money being lent for the purpose of buying raw materials and stocks, and/or for the financing of short-term production costs, and recovered when the end products were sold. It is true that overdrafts were often extended from one year to another, so that in reality the funds may have been used for other purposes than covering periods between expenditure on working-capital items and sale of the product. Also, bridging loans, pending the provision of more permanent capital from other sources, may initially finance longer-term projects.

While traditional forms of lending still predominate, over the last decade the commercial banks have become more disposed to lend on a medium- to long-term basis, rather than just in the form of a regularly reviewed overdraft. In this respect U.K. banks are moving nearer to their European counterparts, which generally provide a much higher proportion of long-term finance for industry than has applied in this country.[14] Long-term lending should not be financed by short-term borrowing, and if the commercial banks were entirely dependent on customers' deposits this more adventurous form of lending would not be possible. These longer bank loans are therefore supported by the banks' ability to borrow in parallel money markets.

As the rate of inflation accelerated during the years 1972–5 reliance on bank borrowing by business increased considerably. This can be seen in Table 3.6, setting out sources of capital funds to U.K. industrial and commercial companies in summary form. There are several reasons for the increased reliance on bank lending. They relate to the fact that profits are no longer sufficient to cover replacement of stocks as their prices rise; nor are they sufficient to provide adequate provision for replacement of assets. The government is apt to react to increasing inflation by imposing more severe taxation, which may not only hit companies directly but also reduce the spendable income of individuals so that it may be difficult for businessmen to raise prices to recoup their costs. Even if the rates of taxation are not raised, the fact that taxation is related to monetary incomes rather than real incomes has meant that business depreciation allowances have been inadequate in relation to cost of replacement and the real income of individuals has been subject to greater taxation as their higher monetary incomes move up into the higher tax ranges. Prices and incomes policy may also mean that many companies have been unable to raise their profits in line with inflation. Superficially it might be thought that in the face of declining real profits, companies might rely to a greater extent on external sources, but a little deeper consideration would dispel this notion; in times of high levels of inflation long-term interest rates can be prohibitive, and, of course, the uncertain profit prospects when inflation shows no signs of abating undermines the market for equity issues. In the circumstances, and bearing in mind the new credit-control arrangements for the banking system which were introduced in 1971 and which meant that bank credit became more freely available, it is not surprising that the figures for bank borrowing show a marked increase.

Table 3.6

Sources of funds of all industrial and commercial companies

| | Per cent of total sources | | | | | | £ million |
	1964	1969	1971	1972	1973	1974	1974
Total internal funds	68·5	72·1	73·4	56·2	55·5	63·3	8026
Bank borrowing	17·2	13·1	12·8	32·9	35·0	34·8	4411
U.K. equity issues for cash	3·6	3·6	2·8	3·6	0·8	0·3	43
Preference share, loan and debenture issues for cash	10·7	11·1	11·1	7·3	8·7	1·6	200
Total sources of funds	100	100	100	100	100	100	12680

Source: *Economic Trends* (September 1975).

Although equity issues appear puny by comparison with other sources, particularly for 1974, it must be remembered that these figures refer to annual sources, not to the total amount of capital outstanding, and that 1974 saw the lowest equity issues for a decade. Also, it should be appreciated that risk capital has an importance beyond its monetary dimension, for it forms the basis for all other forms of capital raising. In other words, it is the foundation for all forms of capital gearing which are built upon it. A company's gearing level will occasionally reach a point where no further loans of any sort may be raised until it has increased its equity base; at that point the raising of, say, £3 million more of loan funds may be entirely dependent on the prior issue of £2 million more equity capital.

Before leaving the topic of provision of funds by the banking sector we must touch briefly on the varied nature of banks and banking services in the United Kingdom. The *clearing banks* have been meeting the challenge of increased competition not only by breaking away somewhat from traditional forms of lending but also by developing new lines of business through subsidiary companies and by participation in such bodies as Finance for Industry, to be referred to at a later point. Thus, through subsidiaries and associated, the clearing banks have now acquired interests in a variety of activities including unit trusts, insurance, factoring, hire purchase, eurocurrencies and credit cards. They have also acquired a stake in the new issue business and, through such subsidiaries as the Barclays Bank Trust Company or Midland Montague Industrial Finance, offer most of the traditional merchant bank services.

The *merchant banks* deserve special mention because they are closely involved in the capital market in a number of ways. Most importantly they are the main advisers to large companies in matters of capital issues. It is in the capacity as issuing houses that they undertake this function. They may initially (in the case of an offer for sale) take up a complete issue but only for the purpose of then offering the shares directly to the investing public. They will advise generally on the form and timing of issues and will undertake such technical matters as arranging for a stock market quotation or preparing a prospectus. They are also managers of pension fund, unit trust and other institutional portfolios, in this way being responsible for investments of over £2000 million. Their services will also often be required by company clients in matters of mergers and takeover bids, and thereby they again exert an important influence in the capital market. Like the clearing banks, they may, in addition to their short-term loans, be prepared to make direct medium- and long-term loans and investments in appropriate instances. Some merchant banks have, for example, been prepared to subscribe for shares in private companies, the aim being to make a large capital profit when, hopefully, the company goes public and gains a quotation at a later date.

Still within the broad area of banking finance come *finance houses* and their leasing and hire-purchase facilities. Generally this is medium-term finance, but leases may run for up to ten years and even fifteen years for major process plant; although hire-purchase contracts are normally for much shorter periods, three years is common for industry and contracts may run up to ten years, with exceptional situations. Specialist suppliers of this form of finance include United Dominions Trust, Mercantile Credit and Bowmaker, but certain merchant banks, including Schroder Wagg, Hambros and Kleinwort Benson also undertake this form of lending.

Yet another form of quasi-bank finance, one which had hardly become established twenty years ago, is that available from the *euro-bond* market. This market supplies currencies other than the domestic currency of the country in which the bank lending the funds (or acting as intermediary for the funds) is located. The primary suppliers of such funds are official institutions, particularly central banks which have built up reserves of foreign currencies, commercial banks, and business and private investors. The funds have usually been available in dollars or Deutsche marks for periods of up to fifteen years. Companies, public corporations and local authorities have borrowed in this way. The foreign currency borrowed may be used as such in the country of its origin, or it may be converted into another currency for use elsewhere. Repayment of the loan has to be made in the currency of issue, and some borrowers who have borrowed at lower interest rates than available at home have lost heavily because of movements in exchange rates between the time of borrowing and the time of repayment.

Official and Specialist Suppliers of Finance

There are so many different sources of finance that it is impracticable to attempt a definitive list or more than a brief account of sources within the confines of this small book; nor is it suggested that the reference to suppliers is in any order of their importance to the market. Suppliers could be regarded as important for many different reasons, for example the size of their funds, the permanence of their lending, the degree of risk involved, the critical importance of the loan to the borrower, or the primary nature of their lending as compared with intermediary lending. The reader who wishes to go into detail and attempt some form of measurement is referred to the reading list at the end of the chapter.

First we will look at a few government or government-backed sources of finance. It is perhaps a debatable point whether government grants form part of the capital market, but they are a source of supply of funds and thus have a bearing on the cost of funds in the market generally. During the period 1966–70 grants were made by the Board of Trade towards the cost of plant and machinery and certain other assets. Regional Development Grants were introduced in the Industry Act of 1972 but are confined to investment by firms within areas of high unemployment, namely Special Development Areas and Development Areas, at present at the rate of 22 and 20 per cent of cost respectively. Within such areas other forms of capital aid may be available; for example, grants towards the cost of removal of plant and machinery, factories built by the Department of Industry for lease on favourable terms, or even grants towards the reduction of interest payments on loans from commercial sources.

The government as a supplier of finance to the public sphere is a subject for a separate study. It makes huge sums available for capital investment in the nationalised industries and to meet their deficits, and via the Public Works Loans Board sums of similar magnitude have been lent to local authorities. (As a rough guide local authorities' and public corporations' borrowing on capital account have averaged in each case £1000 million per annum from central government over the four years to 1974.) As we have indicated on a number of occasions in this book, it is not easy to draw clear dividing lines when discussing capital markets, and the same observation applies to government provision of finance to the public and private spheres. Loans to private industry may end up as loans to public industry. The government guaranteed Rolls Royce's borrowings and eventually took over the aircraft side of the business entirely. Via the Bank of England the government lent money to Burmah Oil in 1974 and soon afterwards, somewhat infamously, bought the B.P. holdings of the Burmah company. To some extent the nature of *ad hoc* government financing may be coloured by the politics of the party in power (though it was the Conservative Government which 'nationalised' Rolls Royce). In 1966 the Labour government established the Industrial Reorganisation Corporation

(I.R.C.) and gave it access to £150 million for the purpose of promoting industrial efficiency by, *inter alia*, acquiring shares, forming companies, making loans and encouraging mergers. The I.R.C. was by no means regarded as an unqualified success and it was disbanded by the Conservative government in 1971. More recently (1974) the Labour government introduced the National Enterprise Board, which bears more than a passing resemblance to the original I.R.C. This new body's functions will include management of any interests taken into public ownership under powers given in the 1972 Industry Act, provision of finance to sound companies which are in temporary financial difficulties, starting new ventures in competition with private enterprise, and/or co-operating with private industry in joint development schemes. The Board is required to supplement and not displace funds from existing sources.

Probably enough has been said to emphasise the interlocking nature of public and private finance, but one further point should be made, and that is that, given a certain level of taxation, any tax allowances relating to capital expenditure which are more generous than depreciation for accounting purposes are a form of government financial assistance. Thus the current 100 per cent first-year capital allowance for plant and machinery, with corporation tax at 52 per cent, amounts to a £52,000 refund on an investment of £100,000. Certainly this could be treated as a form of financial aid in times of stable prices, although with present levels of inflation it could be regarded as a concession to offset the fact that replacement cost accounting for tax purposes has not yet been admitted (it seems that this situation will be remedied).

Finally, before leaving the subject of government-supplied finance, it may be salutary to remind the reader that such finance is derived in the first place largely from the taxation of private individuals and private business. A difference then between publicly and privately supplied finance is that in the former case the suppliers (taxpayers) have no choice about making the funds available; in the latter case the suppliers have a choice as to whether or not to risk their capital. If publicly financed investments turn out to be a failure, the taxpayer is the loser; if privately financed investments fail, those who risked their capital are the losers.

To conclude this chapter we now turn back to a few more independent suppliers of finance (even though in one or two instances the government of the day had a hand in their formation and/or still makes loans available to them).

Finance for Industry (F.F.I.), formed in November 1973 as a holding company, represents a whole network of lenders and investors as their organisation chart (Figure 3.1) indicates. The shareholders in F.F.I. are the English and Scottish clearing banks (85 per cent) and the Bank of England (15 per cent). Although F.F.I. and its operating subsidiaries co-operate with government, it is not a government agency, its funds are not government guaranteed and its subsidiaries do not invest government money. F.F.I. now raises the funds necessary to meet the requirements of its subsidiaries and undertakes the major function of establishing policy. Prior to its formation, both its major operating companies – the Industrial and Commercial Finance Corporation (I.C.F.C.) and the Finance Corporation for Industry (F.C.I.) – had established methods of raising funds, the latter from the clearing banks, the former from a number of sources including share issues, debenture issues, medium- and long-term unsecured loan stock issues, and term deposits from banks. Both the I.C.F.C. and the F.C.I. were originally formed in 1945 to provide business with finance which was not readily obtainable from banks or the new issue market.

I.C.F.C. provides finance for small and medium-sized businesses in amounts ranging from £5000 to £1 million, and since its formation in 1945 it has provided over £375 million of finance to around 3000 U.K. companies. The finance is made available to suit individual needs and may be in the form of secured or unsecured loans, preference, preferred ordinary, or ordinary shares, property and equipment leasing and plant purchase – or a combination of these methods. It does not aim to gain control of a customer's business nor to interfere in management, and although exceptionally it may seek the right to appoint a director to the board, the nominated director will not be a member of I.C.F.C. staff but an independent person. The terms applicable to finance supplied are established by negotiation; for example, loans may be made for periods ranging between ten and twenty years, and repayment, though usually being in annual instalments, can be accelerated by prior agreement. A fixed rate of interest is quoted for the entire period of the loan and is charged on the outstanding amount only. The rates vary according to the security available and the degree of risk, but are reasonable and competitive. The relative importance of

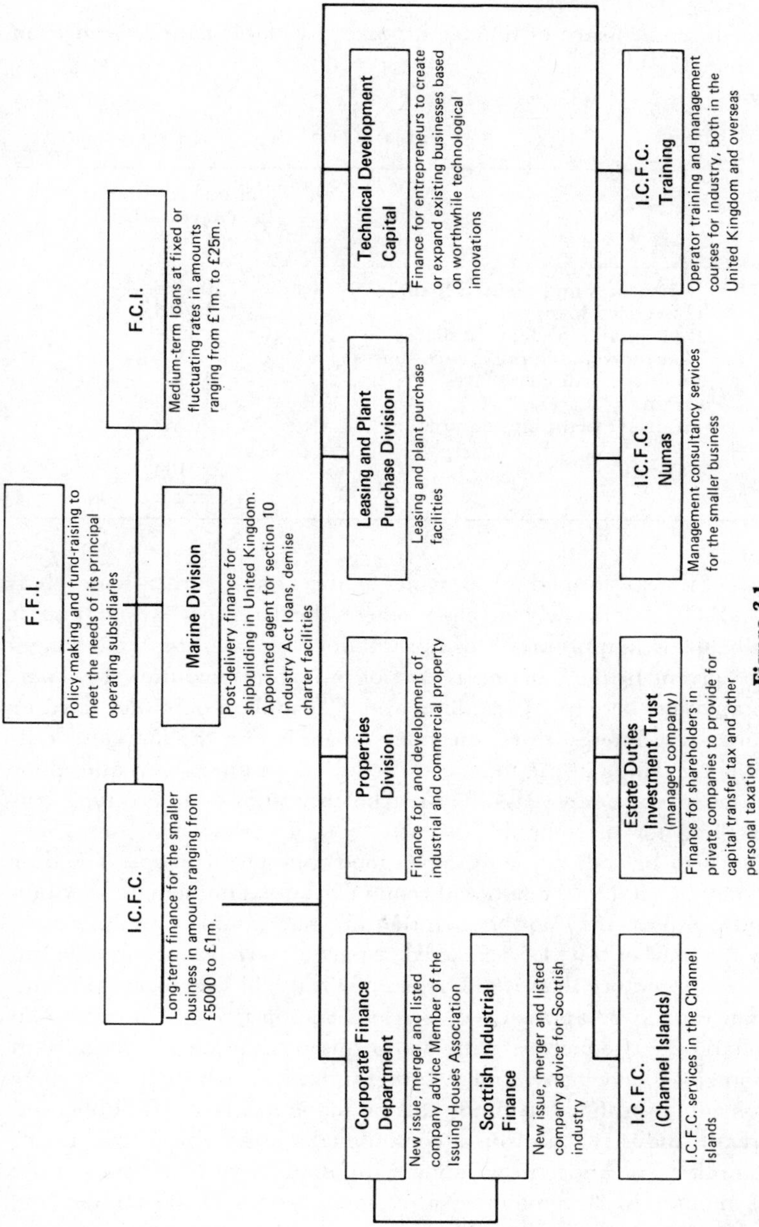

F.F.I.

Policy-making and fund-raising to meet the needs of its principal operating subsidiaries

I.C.F.C.

Long-term finance for the smaller business in amounts ranging from £5000 to £1m.

F.C.I.

Medium-term loans at fixed or fluctuating rates in amounts ranging from £1m. to £25m.

Corporate Finance Department

New issue, merger and listed company advice Member of the Issuing Houses Association

Scottish Industrial Finance

New issue, merger and listed company advice for Scottish industry

Properties Division

Finance for, and development of, industrial and commercial property

Marine Division

Post-delivery finance for shipbuilding in United Kingdom. Appointed agent for section 10 Industry Act loans, demise charter facilities

Leasing and Plant Purchase Division

Leasing and plant purchase facilities

Technical Development Capital

Finance for entrepreneurs to create or expand existing businesses based on worthwhile technological innovations

I.C.F.C. (Channel Islands)

I.C.F.C. services in the Channel Islands

Estate Duties Investment Trust (managed company)

Finance for shareholders in private companies to provide for capital transfer tax and other personal taxation

I.C.F.C. Numas

Management consultancy services for the smaller business

I.C.F.C. Training

Operator training and management courses for industry, both in the United Kingdom and overseas

Figure 3.1

the different forms of finance it makes available can be seen from Table 3.7.

Table 3.7

	Total outstanding at 31 March 1975 ($£$'000)
Debentures and secured loans	106536
Unsecured loans	12815
Redeemable preference shares	8834
Non-redeemable preference shares	2464
Preferred ordinary shares	12409
Ordinary shares	54323
Property, plant and equipment	27753
Total	225134

F.C.I. was formed to provide finance on a larger scale than I.C.F.C., particularly in cases where the customer would find it difficult or inappropriate to raise finance via the Stock Exchange. Its current prime function is that of providing medium-term loans in amounts between £1 million and £25 million on either fixed or fluctuating interest rates, the rates depending on the market conditions prevailing at the time of the loan. Large amounts required for about seven to ten years may not be easy to obtain because this is too long for most banks and too short for insurance companies. The firm or industry may have good long-term prospects and/or it may be vital to the national economy, but its immediate situation and prospects may not be such that an issue would be well received by the market. F.C.I. is expected to play a more positive role within its new structure than it did before 1973; it will seek business rather than wait to be approached as a lender of last resort. It expects to collaborate frequently with nationalised industry, especially in financing heavy investment programmes which will not show immediate profits, but funds will be made available to public and private industry only on a commercially justifiable basis. Loans committed or under negotiation with about sixty companies in the six months to 30 September 1975 amounted to £480 million, the industries concerned including motors and components (£60m.), food and drink (£68m.), engineering (£97m.) and paper, printing and publishing (£55m.).

Two other lending subsidiaries of I.C.F.C. are the Estate Duties Investment Trust Ltd (EDITH) and Technical Development Capital (T.D.C.). The former company was formed in 1952 by I.C.F.C. for the purpose of acquiring minority interests (in the form of ordinary or preference shares) in private or small public companies from shareholders (or their executors) who require funds to meet capital transfer tax or other taxes, such as capital gains tax or the proposed wealth tax. EDITH does not ask for representation on the boards of companies in which it invests, so that the independence of such companies is largely maintained. T.D.C.'s role is that of helping entrepreneurs to create new, or expand existing, businesses based on worthwhile technological innovation. Since its foundation in 1962 it has invested £11 million of high-risk venture capital in such fields as scientific instruments, computer hardware and software, plastics technology and machine tools. It concentrates particularly on developments which are near to commercial realisation and need finance for marketing and production. A minority shareholding combined with a medium-term loan has frequently been found to be the most suitable form of finance provision.

Closely akin to T.D.C. is an independent public corporation, the National Research Development Corporation (N.R.D.C.). Although the N.R.D.C. is not a government department and it does not receive annual grants from the government, it is financed by the Secretary of State for Trade and Industry with government loans. The N.R.D.C. is required to balance its accounts in the long term, and therefore has to conduct its activities on a sound commercial basis. Its main function is to promote the adoption by industry of new products and processes invented in government laboratories, universities and elsewhere, advancing funds as necessary to bring them to a commercially viable stage. About two-thirds of the inventions financed are derived from sources wholly supported by public funds, including the research establishments of the various ministries, the Medical Research Council and the Agricultural Research Council. Private inventions are also supported if the development of such inventions can be regarded as in the public interest. Although the number of inventions accepted from private inventors has been small, a few of them have accounted for some of the N.R.D.C.'s major development projects. Since it was established in 1949, it has sifted nearly 24,000 inventions and about 1300 licence agreements have been negotiated with industry. It has sponsored such diverse projects as the Hovercraft, fuel cells, flexible oil barges (Dracones), antibiotics, potato harvesters, masonry nails (the Loden Anchor) and shrink packaging ('Rapidrap').

The N.R.D.C., in contrast with T.D.C., will support the development stage of a new product as well as the commercial stage; indeed, in special circumstances, it will support applied research where this may lead to an invention. Where appropriate an invention may be placed with industry, a licence being negotiated with the company under the patent rights held by the Corporation; alternatively the N.R.D.C. may participate in joint ventures with industry. The agreement between the N.R.D.C. and a private inventor normally provides for a sharing of the revenue after any development and patent expenditure has been deducted. Although the total expenditure by the N.R.D.C. is not large (less than £50 million on project and patent expenditure over the period 1949–75), by comparison with funds made available by some other suppliers of capital, it is important to appreciate that this is high-risk 'seed capital' which may lead to vast industrial ventures at the later stages.

A number of other suppliers of finance will be mentioned very briefly, although it is not intended to suggest that their importance is in proportion to the few words given to them. Charterhouse Industrial Development Co Ltd provides finance on a somewhat similar basis to the I.C.F.C. It will take up equity shares and make loans to sound companies which have growth prospects, and, unlike the I.C.F.C., it always requires that one of its members shall be represented on the board of the company in which it invests. Other rather smaller investors and lenders of funds include such organisations as Midland Montague Finance, New Court and Partners, Old Broad Street Securities and Safeguard Industrial Investments. Such organisations may amount to a joint venture between financiers (banks or insurance companies) and businesses which are in contact with expanding, well-managed companies. There are a number of organisations too which specialize in providing finance for particular industries, for example the Agriculture Mortgage Corporation (A.M.C.), which provides long-term loans for the purchase of agricultural property, and the Ship Mortgage Finance Company.

The chapter would not be complete without some mention of

finance for industry from E.E.C. sources. These include loans from
the European Investment Bank (E.I.B.) and the European Coal
and Steel Community (E.C.S.C.) re-adaptation and research
grants from the E.C.S.C., grants for training and resettlement from
the European Social Fund; and grants from the European Regional
Development Fund. Because the E.I.B. and the E.C.S.C. can borrow
on international markets on favourable terms, and because they
are non-profit-making institutions, their interest rates tend to
compare favourably with rates from U.K. commercial sources,
but as these loans are largely made available in foreign currency the
exchange risk factor has to be taken into account. The E.I.B. lends
to private and public enterprises for viable projects which fulfil
the broad aims of the Bank, namely contributing to the balanced
development of the Community by making loans towards projects
for (*a*) developing less-developed regions, (*b*) for modernising under-
takings or for developing fresh activities called for the progressive
establishment of the Common Market, and (*c*) forwarding the
common interest of several member states. Most of the loans made
to U.K. enterprises have been for projects in the assisted areas, but
the Bank has also given priority to projects which contribute to an
increase in the E.E.C.'s self-sufficiency in energy. The Bank generally
limits its lending to no more than 40 per cent of the fixed cost of a
project – which are usually large – and most direct loans are for
more than £1 million. It has made loans to such financial intermediaries as the I.C.F.C. in the United Kingdom and has also
assisted with the finance of North Sea gas and oil, nuclear power
and coal projects. The E.C.S.C. makes loans towards investment
programmes concerned directly with coal or steel production, or
those which reduce production costs or improve marketing facilities
(for example harbour installations), or those which may absorb
workers made redundant in the coal or steel industries.

Conclusion

This has been a very wide-ranging if not complete review of the
suppliers of funds. Although the description of these sources has
been supported by figures in some respects, no attempt is made to
compare this assortment of lenders and investors in numerical terms
in this brief summary. Such an exercise would be grossly misleading.
Not only is there a good deal of overlapping and interlocking among

the assortment listed, but the survey has covered several different types of financial provision; for example, short-to-medium-term lending, well-secured or guaranteed; long-term lending, secured and unsecured; investment in sound, well-established concerns; investment in young but go-ahead companies; high-risk investment in ideas and ventures; and grants for desirable projects and industries. It may well be thought that a modest provision of finance in quantitative terms may nevertheless be of vital importance when it happens to be the only source which can be tapped and which is critical to the growth of firm and/or industry. On the other hand, at the shorter end of the market, where alternative suppliers are competing with each other and loans are more frequently redeemed, the vast sums of money outstanding may appear to somewhat over-rate the importance of this finance.

Any comparative survey in quantitative terms might also appear to underestimate the importance of the individual saver. Banks, insurance companies, pensions funds and other financial intermediaries tend to dominate the supply side of the capital market, but it must be remembered that the credit and finance supplied by these institutions is built upon individual savings, and even government sources of finance, far from being free or independent, are derived either from the taxable capacity of the people or from their willingness to invest in government securities. Whether funds are supplied direct to industry by individuals or supplied indirectly through intermediaries of one sort or the other, the users of such funds should be aware of the root source and of their heavy responsibility to make optimum use of the finance put at their disposal.

Further Reading

D. J. Baum and N. B. Stiles, *The Silent Partners* (Syracuse University Press, 1965).

R. J. Briston, *The Stock Exchange and Investment Analysis* (London: Allen & Unwin, 1975).

K. Midgley, *Companies and their Shareholders – the Uneasy Relationship* (Institute of Chartered Secretaries and Administrators, 1975).

Royal Commission on the Distribution of Wealth, *Reports Nos 1 and 2*, Cmnd. 6171/2 (London: H.M.S.O., 1975).

R. Dobbins and M. J. Greenwood, 'Institutional Shareholders and

Equity Market Stability', *Journal of Business Finance and Accounting*,
  vol. 2, no. 2 (Summer 1975).
R. Dobbins and T. W. McRae, *Institutional Shareholders and Corporate
  Management* (Bradford: M.C.B. Journals, 1975).
Various publications by commercial and public lending bodies can
be obtained direct from the bodies concerned, for example:

The Stock Exchange Financial Information Services,
The Public Relations Department,
The Stock Exchange, London EC2N 1HP.

Finance for Industry Ltd, (and I.C.F.C. and EDITH)
91 Waterloo Road, London SE1 8XP.

National Research Development Corporation,
Kingsgate House,
66–74 Victoria Street,
London SW1E 6SL.

The Charterhouse Group Ltd,
1 Paternoster Row,
St Pauls, London EC4P 4HP.

CHAPTER 4

The Demand for Capital: New Equipment, its Operation and Finance

In this chapter we examine some of the internal processes and logic applied in organisations which lead to their demand for capital. We mainly discuss a commercial environment, but others are also referred to. The chapter is divided into four sections which deal with: the internal *processes* involved with capital expenditure decisions; the techniques utilised when *evaluating proposals;* principles involved when choosing the type of *finance for capital expenditure;* and the principles used when *financing the operations* following capital expenditure.

The Processes of Capital Expenditure

BACKGROUND STUDY

The events leading to payments for new assets will obviously vary from one organisation to another, but each will incorporate certain fundamentals in its processes. For example, every organisation must have *a system for bringing forward the new ideas* and various other claimants for a share of its capital budget. When the claims for funds have been formalised, the next major stage in the capital-expenditure process is evaluation and decision, and this will be performed by an individual or group of individuals who has the power to sanction or refuse such expenditure. Also, there must be somewhere in the organisation another group who will try to ensure that there is a supply of finance available to fund the purchase of assets and their operation.

Most organisations of any size have internal procedures that require a formal application to be made for finance for capital expenditure, and they will have pre-printed forms for that purpose.

Such forms have a variety of names and a common one is a 'capital-expenditure requisition'. Applicants are usually required to give an outline of the project envisaged and a list of its costs and benefits. The latter are then perused by the decision-makers and compared with some investment criteria provided by the highest authority within the organisation.

Exactly who the decision-makers are will depend upon the size of the capital expenditure. Small amounts are usually sanctioned at a modest level in the management hierarchy, whereas large projects require examination and approval by the top executives. Those senior executives will also want to ensure that they have some over-all control of the total of smaller capital expenditures, so they often delegate authority for small sums up to a defined sum in aggregate.

Earlier we mentioned that applicants for capital expenditure should be able to demonstrate to sanctioning authorities that certain investment criteria have been met. In commercial organisations, criteria are usually set in terms of a rate of profit or of excess of cash inflows over cash outflows. There are a number of factors which will influence the size of profits, etc. required, and these include the following: the rate of interest paid on money borrowed to finance the project; the rate of profit recently earned by the company; the rate of profit being earned by competitors; the return expected by the owners, and in turn that will be influenced by what they could earn with their money if it were invested elsewhere; and the expected rate of inflation.

Nationalised industries have huge capital-expenditure pro-grammes, and those industries are also normally expected to demonstrate the likelihood of a satisfactory return in commercial terms before sanctioning new investment projects. But the economic value of investments made by nationalised industries cannot always be evaluated only by reference to the more obvious *financial* return to that industry. Many of their investments produce social costs and benefits which in principle can have financial values placed upon them, and these, it is argued, should be taken into account when seeking to make or refute economic justification for capital ex-penditure. For example, modern extensions to the London under-ground train transport system are put forward as cases where the social benefit from the relief of congestion should feature in economic evaluations of those projects.

From what has been said in the previous paragraph, it is apparent that decisions on capital-expenditure proposals in the public sector are affected to varying extents by the estimated value to the community of such projects. Whereas nationalised industries, new projects will on occasions have some features on which it is difficult to place financial values, other non-trading areas of the public sector must have vast amounts of capital expenditure which are almost incapable of being evaluated in a similar manner to that which applies to the commercial private sector. New schools and defence projects are just two categories having a substantial appetite for capital expenditure where criteria for screening are different from those in industry. Political benefit, relief of unemployment or taxation, and national security, all are factors which may be considered.

So far no mention has been made of the fairly obvious constraint imposed on capital expenditure by the supply of finance. The over-all supply will often impose a maximum to capital expenditures, and the criteria mentioned in the preceding paragraphs will provide the means for choosing between the various competitors for a share of that total. The factors influencing the size of that total will be diverse, and at their head, or close thereto, will be the various facets of government policy. For example, such policy or changes thereto will affect the financial institutions' appraisal of an industry's economic prospects. There are also a variety of internal factors such as management's willingness, or aversion, to sharing control and incurring debt.

EXAMPLES OF BUSINESS PRACTICE

It is proposed in this section to give examples of the processes employed as is evidenced by reports on individual companies and as revealed by various research works. The first of these examples is interesting in that it recounts the early procedures for capital-expenditure appraisal systems at General Motors via the memories of one of its chiefs:[1]

Effecting Corporate Control: Appropriations for Capital Spending (time 1919)

The core of our concept lay in the determination of the propriety of proposed projects. Four principles were to be satisfied, which we stated as follows:

a) Is the Project a logical or necessary one considered as a commercial venture?

b) Has the Project been properly developed technically?

c) Is the Project proper, considering the interest of the Corporation as a whole?

d) What is the relative value of the Project to the Corporation as compared with other Projects under consideration, from the standpoint not only of the return on the necessary capital to be invested, but of the need of the particular Project in supporting the operation of the Corporation, as a whole?

We allowed certain small amounts of expenditure to be authorised by the general manager of a division on his own. For larger amounts we proposed a detailed procedure on the development and follow-up of supporting data.

A separate review and sanctioning authority examined such items.
. . . an appropriations manual (was) developed for the corporation setting forth in detail the kind of information the divisions and subsidiaries should present to demonstrate the desirability of a proposed expenditure both from an engineering and economic standpoint.

Proper records were to be kept of expenditures and approvals for expenditures, and uniform treatment was to be given to appropriation requests throughout the corporation. . . . After that it would be a matter of business judgement whether to grant a request.

(Changes in this procedure have been made from time to time. . . . However, in its essentials, this is still the way capital appropriations are approved in General Motors.)

It is interesting to see that so often in company accounts of their capital-expenditure processes they head their description in terms of *control* rather than *decision-making*. That was the case in the General Motors record above, and can be seen to apply in the papers delivered by executives of Unilever Limited, and the Dunlop Rubber Company Limited, from which extracts are reproduced below. It should not necessarily be assumed that because of this there is more emphasis on caution and avoidance of wrong decisions than on the more adventurous aspects of risk-taking.

The next company process we are going to use as illustrative is taken from an article on 'Decentralisation in Unilever Limited'.[2]

Control

In Unilever, control from the centre rests upon three devices: the Annual Operating Plan, the Annual Capital Expenditure Budget, and the Appointment and Remuneration of Top Management.

The Capital Expenditure Budget. This includes all items on which it can be foreseen that money will have to be spent during the year – renewals of, and repairs to existing plant, and additional plant where required – for the current operating plan or to provide for expected future demand. It might also include a suggestion for the acquisition of a business if that were considered the most economical method of bringing about a desired development. The instrument is, therefore, the means of focusing medium and long-term policy, because almost every long-term policy will require capital expenditure in some form. It is appropriate, therefore, that this budget should be discussed with deliberation, and the views of a number of Advisory and Service Departments are likely to be sought.

The control of capital expenditure is more centralised than that of current operation. The operating units, National Managements, Executives and Technical Division, have discretion to spend up to certain limits; but above these limits all capital expenditures have to be authorised by the Board, because control of capital expenditure will only be effective if it is carried out by a Central agency able to look at the whole field of the concern's interest, existing and potential, in relation to the resources available or likely to become available.

The last of these extracts is interesting because, in addition to emphasising how big companies seek to control their financial affairs, there is the indication that capital expenditure is varied up and down in size in the short term to match the surplus cash flow generated from current operations. The extract is from a paper on 'Integration by Administration' at the Dunlop Rubber Company.[3]

Budgets provide a means for overseeing, directing and controlling activities from Head Office.

Throughout the group, in every unit at home and overseas, there is budgetary control[4] sub-divided in the main between capital budgets and profit and loss accounts. The capital budget is again sub-divided between long-term forecasts, which are usually annually revised estimates for the following five years, and annual budgets with quarterly revisions. The annual capital budgets are revised quarterly, particularly because they have an important impact on the cash budget, which also covers working capital.

Research and personal observations have demonstrated that there is much more to capital-expenditure decision-making than mechanical application of systems which proceed through stages of generating requisitions, quantitative analysis of cost and revenue implications, examination of net outcome with some criteria and, if approval is given, the allocation of finance. There is of course the expected range, between companies, of the years ahead over which they forecast such variables as market size and shares, and there are also variations in the thoroughness of the preparation of data for such decisions.[5]

But what really needs to be remembered is that the summary in this paragraph can be viewed as a skeleton which is given flesh and blood by personalities involved. It seems, for example, that in giant firms decisions on important, large capital expenditures may be taken by a few individuals, and in cases where the Chairman or Managing Director is a dominant individual such decisions can rest with a single person.[6]

There are also many hints of a lack of objectivity and making do with subjective methods in the processes leading to capital-expenditure approval in practice. (Note that there are also many examples of the reverse, which are less newsworthy.) Barna, for example, found that 'In some large electrical firms it was particularly clear that some investment decisions were not determined by relative profitability or an attempt to concentrate resources on the most successful fields.'[7] Such views are given support in various places. For example, a company secretary of A.E.I. said in a paper he delivered:[8]

Our domestic appliance business had been on the down-grade for years. . . . . This was not the fault of the men who worked for

Hotpoint; *we had always regarded ourselves as a heavy engineering company*, and what money there was for capital development had gone to the heavy side of the business, to the starvation of the appliance side.

Williams and Scott have also reported what can be construed as an apparent lack of objectivity.[9] 'The likelihood of a gradual commitment to a project *before* investigation and evaluation are complete is even greater when "policy issues" are involved. . . . It could require very unfavourable evidence to destroy the project.'

POSSIBLE FUTURE CHANGES

It is possible that in the next decade there will occur some major changes in the decision-making processes concerning capital expenditure. It seems likely that decision-makers might include representatives of work-forces (as well as the management of course), and that there may be more consultation with government. The pressures for participation are coming from organised labour (although not all trade unions support the idea because to some trade unionist decision-making is a *management* problem) and from the Labour government. However, it seems likely that the trend will be for workers to join supervisory boards. Such boards would probably not have a direct say in capital-expenditure decision-making, but they might have some power of veto.

There are examples of moves towards appointing 'worker directors', who will presumably have some say in capital-expenditure discussions, and the troubled motor industry provides illustrations of this at British Leyland and Chrysler. For those organisations which move in this direction there will be interesting problems concerning changes (or no change) in the *real* people making decisions, and in bridging the dichotomy between democratic and speedy decisions.

As far as the future relationship between industry's capital expenditure and government is concerned, it is possible that companies in regional areas will be offered some financial benefits if they enter into 'planning agreements' with ministers. Such arrangements will concern those future developments over a specified period which would in the opinion of the minister contribute to national needs and objectives. Also, certain larger companies may find in the near future that they are required to disclose information to government ministers concerning, amongst other things, the undertaking's capital expenditure. The Industry Act legislation extends to requiring estimates of the future and to providing such information to trade unions.

After these changes are introduced it seems unlikely that when the information is provided to the work-force and their representatives, the latter will remain completely passive. It seems reasonable to suppose that before very long these new proposals will be accompanied by changes in some of the procedures for setting policies and making decisions on capital expenditures. Probably, however, we are still some way short of features of the French system which includes provisions for allocating the supply of capital to companies on the basis of national benefits as outlined in the National Plan.

Techniques for Evaluating Capital Expenditure

We are now going to examine that stage in the capital-expenditure decision process which involves analysing a proposal, comparing it with a minimum economic requirement, and making a decision on the economic merits. First, it is convenient to explain that businessmen in both public and private sectors set the economic requirement in terms either of a pay-off or pay-back period, or in a way related to the percentage return on the investment. In the latter case the percentage may relate to the original cost of the capital expenditure or some varying amount which takes into account the reduction in value of the original expenditure. Modern practices in larger organisations ask of their analyst: 'Will this project earn our minimum earnings requirement of x per cent?' Alternatively, they ask: 'What percentage return will this project earn?' That forecast earnings rate is then compared with their x per cent minimum requirement. The various factors which will determine the size of x were discussed at the start of this chapter.

At this stage it is necessary to resort to some arithmetic in order to understand how modern practice calculates the *percentage* return of forecast profits on proposed capital expenditure. It is not as straightforward as one would wish and entails the application of discounting techniques. Forecast profits in our examples can be defined as the annual totals of the difference between cash inflows and cash outflows directly generated by the projects being considered.

THE MECHANICS OF DISCOUNTING[10]

Let us assume that the finance necessary to purchase capital equipment has to be borrowed from someone or some financial institution at a cost of 10 per cent. Further, let us assume that any cash flows (that is, an excess of the project's annual inflows over its outflows) will be used as they accrue to pay back part of the original borrowings necessary to finance the project, and to pay interest thereon. It will therefore be apparent that earlier receipts will be more beneficial than late receipts of the same size because they can repay borrowings earlier and save more interest cost.

Now let us set up a problem – Problem (1) – namely: 'Is it worth paying out £10,000 on a project if it has annual net cash flows for each of the next three years of £4000 p.a. ?' Or, put another way, does the project's annual cash flows repay its capital cost and satisfy a minimum earnings requirement of 10 per cent p.a., which is the annual cost of the capital to be borrowed to finance the project?

The problem can be solved fairly easily using discounting techniques. Such techniques charge the annual cash flows with compound interest from the date of borrowing to the date of receiving the annual amount. (Note that although receipts will usually accrue throughout a year, they are deemed to arrive on one date at the end of the year for ease of calculation.)

Those annual cash flows, now net of interest charges, are then aggregated to ascertain whether in total they are sufficient to repay the original loan. Fortunately there are tables which enable us to apply factors which automatically remove the interest charge from future cash flows to leave a remainder, known as the present value of those flows. Those remainders are in total the amount of original loan which could be repaid and serviced with interest from the project's annual returns. Such a table is provided in the Appendix (pp. 135–6), and has been used below to provide the factors 0·909 etc. in the solution to our simple problem.

SOLUTION TO PROBLEM (1)

A receipt of £4000 at the end of year 1 repays a 10 per cent loan of £4000 × 0·909, that is, repays a loan of £3636 granted at the beginning.

A receipt of £4000 at the end of year 2 repays a 10 per cent loan of £4000 × 0·826, that is repays a loan of £3304 granted at the beginning.

A receipt of £4000 at the end of year 3 repays a 10 per cent loan of £4000 × 0·751, that is repays a loan of £3004 granted at the beginning.

Therefore, the stream of future cash flows inwards could repay a loan of £3636 + £3304 + £3004 = £9944 and service it with interest at 10 per cent p.a. on the balances of the loan outstanding; but they are not sufficient to repay the loan of £10,000 required to finance the project. Therefore this project should not be sanctioned.

A common method for showing the above workings is produced in Table 4.1, and that format will be used elsewhere in the remainder of this chapter.

Table 4.1

Year 0 Capital expenditure (financed with 10 per cent capital)	£10000
Year 1 Cash flow 4000 × 0·909 (factor for 10 per cent at 1 year)	= £3636
2 ,, ,, 4000 × 0·826	= £3304
3 ,, ,, 4000 × 0·751	= £3004
	£9944

Conclusion: rejected because present value of returns are less than project cost.

Now let us apply this technique to a slightly more involved problem where we have to determine the size of the cash flows to which the discount factors should be applied. Subsequently, we will examine the effect on the project's viability of any uncertainties we may have about the project's future performance, costs and revenues.

PROBLEM (2) THE FURNITURE MANUFACTURER

The project considered in this simple example is that of a civil servant who has decided to set up a small business for a limited period of time rather than continue with his employment. We are ignoring inflation, pensions and taxation to ease the complexity.

The financial details of his plan are shown in Table 4.2 and cover the four years for which he envisages he will want to stay in business. He estimates that he will sell the equipment at the end of year 4 for £600 and that his salary during those four years would be £4000, £4500, £5000 and £6000 (the same as for his Civil Service position).

Table 4.2

Various capital equipment including a vehicle	£2000
Sales: Year 1	£6000
Years 2–4	£12000 p.a.
Costs: varying with volume, that is, variable costs – mainly materials (a quote for which has been obtained) – will amount to one-third of sales revenue	
Costs: independent of volume, that is, fixed costs	£1000 p.a.

The initial finances required would be drawn from his deposit account which yields 12 per cent p.a. That withdrawal would amount to £3000 made up of the following: equipment £2000, and working capital £1000 (that is, to finance initial materials £400 and early wages £600).

Question: Do you advise undertaking this project?

SOLUTION TO PROBLEM (2)

Initial analysis suggests the above project would need to earn at least 12 per cent p.a., which is the interest rate forgone by withdrawing £3000 from the deposit account. Indeed, the entrepreneur might require more than 12 per cent p.a. because this project has greater risks than those associated with his deposit. Our workings, shown in Table 4.3, indicate that the project earns enough to repay a withdrawal of over £4300, whereas only £3000 is required. It appears to be a good thing. In fact you will see we calculate the return to be somewhat over 26 per cent.

Table 4.3

Discounted cash flow: furniture manufacturer

Year	Outflow (£)				Inflow (£)		Net (£)
0	Equipment and Working Capital			3000			−3000
	VC[(a)]	FC[(b)]	Salary	Total	Sales etc.	Total	
1	2000[(c)] +	1000 +	3400[(d)]	6400	6000, i.e. sales	6000	−400
2	4000 +	1000 +	4500	9500	12000	12000	2500
3	4000 +	1000 +	5000	10000	12000	12000	2000
4	4000 +	1000 +	6000	11000	12000 + 400[(e)] + 600[(f)]	13000	2000

Discounted at 12 per cent   *and at 26 per cent*[h]

Year 1	-400×0.893 [g]	$=$	-357	0.794	-318 [g]
Year 2	$+2500 \times 0.797$	$=$	1992	0.630	1575
Year 3	$+2000 \times 0.712$	$=$	1424	0.500	1000
Year 4	$+2000 \times 0.636$	$=$	1272	0.397	794

£4331   3051

Initial withdrawal from
deposit account   £3000

Therefore the project appears to permit approval.

Points on workings: (a) variable costs; (b) fixed costs; (c) 1/3 × £6000 sales revenue; (d) salary in year 1, £4000, less £600 financed from deposit account; (e) the release of the initial capital tied up in materials – this could alternatively be shown as a reduction in the £4000 variable cost in year 4; (f) from the sale of equipment; (g) discount factors from Appendix 1; (h) determined after trial and error as the interest rate which reduces the future cash flows in aggregate to an amount similar to the project cost – this is the method of determining the rate of return the project actually earns.

Problem (2) to this point has introduced a number of new points and the more important can thus be summarised:

(i) The interest rate used can either be the cost of servicing capital used (as in problem (1)) or the rate of interest forgone, the rate on the deposit account in problem (2);

(ii) Project finance is required both for new equipment – capital expenditure – and for working capital. In practice the proportion of working capital might be higher than in this problem and is often substantially underestimated.

(iii) We can calculate a project's rate of return by finding by trial-and-error methods the rate of discount interest to be applied to future cash flows to reduce them to an account equal to the project's initial cost.

Let us now return to the problem. It appears that a return of 26 per cent in replacement of interest forgone at 12 per cent is a worthwhile proposition. (And remember earnings equal to that in the Civil Service post have been charged to the project.) However, this viability is dependent upon reasonable accuracy in the various forecasts. There is a sufficient history and documentation of errors in forecasts to encourage even the most adventurous to exercise caution.[11] Therefore let us have a look at the forecasts made in problem (2), and ask ourselves how uncertain we are about each. These are shown in Table 4.4.

Table 4.4

The uncertainties

Initial outflow	Fairly certain, quotations will have been obtained
Material costs	Fairly certain initially, there has been a quote
Other costs	The non-variable will probably include a high proportion for rent which could have been fixed for a longish period. Some other costs will be uncertain, for example vehicle maintenance
Salary	Fairly certain if it is to be aligned to his Civil Service salary
Resale value of equipment	Uncertain, but relatively small amount
Sales volume	Uncertain
Selling price	This is very related to sales volume, could be fairly certain because it is agreed to/set by owner
Discount rate	Fairly uncertain. Deposit rates are related to Bank Rate which tends to vary, and risk differential should be considered

After examining the data we are likely to feel that the most uncertain aspect of the project is the sales revenue. Our entrepreneur would be well advised to test whether a relatively small error in sales revenue, or anything else, could have a relatively large effect on the economic viability of his project. The effect of demand being 10 per cent less than that forecast in the example would reduce net inflows to: −800, 1700, 1200, 1200 (remember that to arrive at these figures, only variable costs and sales need to be changed of the outflows and inflows in our previous detailed workings).

	Discounted at 12 per cent		*Discounted at 5 per cent*	
Year 1	− 800 × 0·893	−714	0·952	−762
Year 2	+1700 × 0·797	1355	0·907	1542
Year 3	+1200 × 0·712	854	0·864	1037
Year 4	+1200 × 0·636	763	0·823	988
		2258		2805

This project which cost £3000 indicates less than a break-even position if only the alternative sales forecast were achieved. In fact, the project then would earn less than 5 per cent.

Such an approach to testing the effects of errors in forecasts is known as 'sensitivity analysis', and when applied to this problem could easily persuade the entrepreneur not to proceed with the project.

Both discounting procedures and sensitivity analysis are becoming more common techniques amongst larger organisations both public and private. For example, some of the methods used by the national-ised industry sector are quoted below:[12]

> The Government expects the nationalised industries to use the best methods of appraisal. Discounted cash flow techniques, which are already widely used by the nationalised industries, are recommended for all important projects.
>
> Whenever possible, estimates should be made of the likely range of outcomes, and investment undertaken only when management judges that prospects are, on balance, favourable.
>
> But all projects need to be assessed in a systematic way allowing for uncertainties in the forecasts of demand and of technological development.

If one is going to do several recalculations of a project's return for a number of possibilities, a range of possible returns will be produced, and one must take care that the presentation of this range is not unwieldy. Graphical presentations are often the clearest and the example (Figure 4.1) shows what the returns would be with a number of alternative outcomes from a project to produce a chemical plant. A key to the points plotted is provided.

Key to points plotted in Figure 4.1

S_{10} Basic sales estimate; plant life 15 years, 20 years, 25 years.

S_{11} Basic sales estimate $+10$ per cent; plant life, 15, 20, 25 years.

S_{12} Basic sales estimate -10 per cent; plant life, 15, 20, 25 years.

R_{10} Reduction in plant specification (and hence in capital cost). Basic sales estimate; plant life 15, 20 years (no 25 years because of degradation of specification).

R_{11} As R_{10} but with sales 10 per cent higher.

R_{12} As R_{10} but with sales 10 per cent lower.

R_{20} The return on a modification which costs £275,000 but creates an annual cash saving of 2 per cent on costs; plant life 15, 20, 25 years.

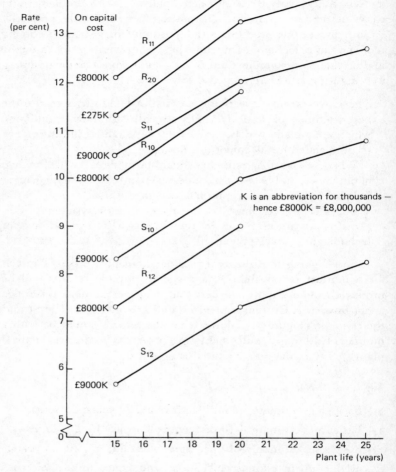

Figure 4.1   *Summary graph of D.C.F. yields on proposed project taking into account certain major variables (Emsport Chemicals)*

The management at Emsport Chemicals would probably draw a horizontal line across the graph to represent the minimum return required, and then they would have to make judgements about the probability of achieving the situations with plots above that cut-off line.

When dealing with capital-expenditure appraisals which cover periods of anticipated inflation, there are in practice a variety of approaches. However, we recommend here that the way to incorporate estimated inflation into the appraisal is to include its effects on forecasts of annual costs and annual revenues, and to charge against those annual revenues in the last year of operation the increase in the replacement cost over the original cost of assets retired. In that way the real capital of the organisation should be maintained. The practice in inflationary times of charging supplementary depreciation over and above that calculated on the original cost of assets is a common procedure of modern accounting methods in organisations, and its counterpart in investment appraisal will be recognised in the recommendations mentioned above. An illustration of how those recommendations might be applied is given in Problem (3) below.

PROBLEM (3)   TRANSPORT COMPANY

A transport company is considering undertaking an expansion. It is anticipated that the new project will last for four years, the life of the additional vehicles, and that further work of this kind would develop thereafter.

The estimated cost of vehicles now is £50,000 and net operating cash flow, that is cash inflow less cash outflow from operations, before finance charges will be £10,000, £20,000, £20,000 and £15,000. These amounts are all before U.K. inflation, which is estimated at 20, 22, 18 and 15 per cent for the relevant years.

The owner anticipates that his operating margins and net cash flow can keep pace with inflation, but that the replacement cost of vehicles will escalate at a lower rate due to the increasing competition from the Japanese commercial lorry industry. He forecasts the rate of increase in lorry prices over the four years to be 18, 15, 15 and 12 per cent.

A £50,000 overdraft facility can be obtained at 16 per cent p.a. (At the time of preparing this example these inflation rates and interest rate were current or reasonable expectations. Although the rates will change the principles should remain.)

On the basis of these figures, is the project economically viable?

The problem can be tackled via a number of schedules which are now provided.

Schedule 1

Adjusting operating cash flows for inflation

Year	Cash flow before inflation (£000)	Inflation adjustment factor	Cash flow after inflation (£000)
1	10	1·20 (i.e. 1·00 × 1·20)	12·0
2	20	1·46 (i.e. 1·20 × 1·22)	29·2
3	20	1·73 (i.e. 1·46 × 1·18)	34·6
4	15	1·99 (i.e. 1·73 × 1·15)	29·8

Schedule 2

Calculating replacement cost of vehicles

Year	Cost (£000)	Inflation adjustment factor	Replacement cost (£000)
0	50	1·00	
1		1·18 (i.e. 1·00 × 1·18)	
2		1·36 (i.e. 1·18 × 1·15)	
3		1·56 (i.e. 1·36 × 1·15)	
4		1·75 (i.e. 1·56 × 1·12)	87·5 (i.e. 50 × 1·75) i.e. an extra 37·5

Schedule 3

Test whether the project earns 16 per cent p.a.

Year	Inflated cash flow (sch. 1) (£000)	Extra replacement cost (sch. 2) (£000)	Discount factor	Present value (£000)
1	12		0·862	12·0 × 0·862 = 10·3
2	29·2		0·743	29·2 × 0·743 = 21·7
3	34·6		0·641	34·6 × 0·641 = 22·2
4	29·8	37·5	0·552	−7·7 × 0·552 = −4·3
				49·9
			PROJECT COST	50·0

Thus this project demonstrates that by the end of year 4 it can finance the extra cost of replacing the old vehicles, and that the remaining cash flows have a present value (that is, a value after deducting interest charges) of approximately the same amount as the project's capital cost. It is marginally viable.

Those who prefer to check the arithmetic by looking forward in time to examine whether the project will have both paid off the £50,000 overdraft, and provided the extra £37,500 in replacement cost of the vehicles by the end of year 4, should be reassured by schedule 4.

Schedule 4

Effect of project on the overdraft facility (£000)

Balance at beginning of year	Interest adjustment at 16 per cent opening balance	Cash flow adjustment (sch. 1)	Balance at end of year
Year 1 o/d 50 +	8	− 12	= o/d 46
2 o/d 46 +	7·4	− 29·2	= o/d 24·2
3 o/d 24·2 +	3·1*	− 34·6	= cr 7·3 + 0·2†
4 cr 7·5 +	1·2	+ 29·8	= cr 38·5
	Less extra cost of replacement		37·5
			1·0

Note: o/d = overdraft; cr = credit balance.
* 16 per cent on 24·2 for, say, 80 per cent of year.
† 16 per cent on 7·3 for, say, 20 per cent of year.

Both schedules 3 and 4 demonstrate that on a first screening the project is marginally satisfactory. (Many of the features necessary for a real life screening, for example taxation, changing interest rates on overdraft and sensitivity analysis have been omitted for simplicity.) Should inflation have been ignored altogether in this example, we would have rejected the proposition as not satisfying a 16 per cent earnings rate, as is shown in schedule 5.

Schedule 5

Test whether the project earns 16 per cent p.a. – inflation ignored

Year	Cash flow (£000)	Discount factor	Present value (£000)
1	10	0·862	8·6
2	20	0·743	14·9
3	20	0·641	12·8
4	15	0·552	8·3
			44·6
		PROJECT COST	50·0

But should we have incorporated inflation in the cash-flow estimates, but omitted charging the extra costs involved in replacing the vehicles, we would have had the mistaken impression of a project with a substantial margin over the 16 per cent earnings rate required, as is shown in Schedule 6.

Schedule 6

Test whether the project earns 16 per cent – inflation included in cash flows, but omitting the extra replacement cost

Year	Inflated cash flow (sch. 1) (£000)	Discount factor	Present value (£000)
1	12	0·862	10·3
2	29·2	0·743	21·7
3	34·6	0·641	22·2
4	29·8	0·552	16·4
			70·6
		PROJECT COST	50·0

What we have tried to do in the above illustrations is to demonstrate how inflationary effects on operating costs, operating revenues and replacement capital expenditure can be included in capital-expenditure appraisals. We have sought to demonstrate how one may attempt *to maintain the real value of the capital of* the business and its owners. In more realistic circumstances the rate of interest on capital borrowed might vary from year to year, and this could be accommodated in the investment appraisal by changing the interest rate from year to year to bring it in line with the interest rate forecast to be charged during those years. The application would be straightforward when applying the method shown in schedule 4, but for the discounting approach it would be better to use the weighted average interest rate as a guide to the discount rate.

If the capital expenditure were financed from the owner's personal funds he might expect his annual return from those funds to take account of inflation. (Government regulation of dividends will be the complicating factor to be observed in practice.) Exactly how this expectation should be built into a project appraisal is a matter of disagreement between those who attempt to postulate an answer.[13] Maintenance of the real value of owner's capital has already been incorporated but we have still to examine the maintenance of their income.

A useful starting point is to examine how the cost of owner's funds (return expected on owner's funds) can be determined, because there is no contractual rate to provide a simple answer as is the case with, say, loans. About the most straightforward approach to this is to say the rate of owner's return required is an amount somewhat greater than the yield on risk-free capital, for example government stock. The size of that premium will be determined by the level of risk to which owners are subject; but the market yield on government stock tends to take account of future expected price changes.[14] Hence, if the return required on owner's funds is based on the return on government stock, the former must already have built into it an amount to compensate for future inflation. Therefore, when appraising projects to be financed wholly or partly with risk capital, the discount rate is likely to be determined on a basis which has already incorporated an allowance for inflation, and some authorities says that normally no further allowance should be included.[15] However, the logic of this is difficult to accept in times when the inflation rate exceeds interest rates on government stock. A pragmatic approach is to accept that the interest rate on government stock includes two aspects, namely a basic interest of around 5 per cent and an allowance for inflation. The supplier of risk capital/owner's capital might therefore require 5 per cent + a risk premium + the expected inflation rate. Forecast changes in the inflation rate could be incorporated by a procedure which is very similar to that for dealing with expected changes in interest rates on bank borrowing, a procedure which was described earlier.

Financing Capital Expenditure

Perhaps the most obvious constraint on capital expenditure is the availability of money with which to finance it. However, for the remaining part of this section we will make the assumption that finance is available and the only problems we have to solve concern choice from among the very many different types of finance on offer. We will proceed in three parts, in which we discuss broad influences on our choice. Those influences are: the basic choice between long-term and short-term finance; whether the finance used for capital expenditure should be supplied from surpluses on existing operations (internally generated) or should come from a source external to the company (for example a share issue); and third the costs of various different sorts of capital.

We will see that the cost aspect cannot be confined to its compartment but will infiltrate the other areas so that, for example, the choice between long-term capital and short-term capital will be influenced by cost considerations.

Finally, we remind readers that a variety of suppliers of finance are discussed in chapter 3.

LONG-TERM/SHORT-TERM CONSIDERATIONS

There is an old adage in financial circles that it can be extremely risky to finance long-term assets with short-term money. Capital expenditure is money spent on long-term assets, that is, assets which organisations will want to own for several years. Short-term money is finance provided for a short period only. It is money that may require repayment before the long-term assets have completed their life. The basis of the adage is that many organisations have come to grief because their supply of short-term money has been withdrawn and could be repaid only after an expensive realisation of the long-term assets they were financing. When building something like a brewery, it is more reassuring to know it is being financed with money lent for say twenty years, than if it were built with money renewable/returnable at six months notice. In the latter case it may be very difficult to find the cash with which to repay the financier should he exercise his option to recall his money. It could certainly prove difficult to sell a semi-complete brewery to provide the necessary liquid resources (Apologies!). The problem could be much more severe if the building was more specialist, perhaps a chemical plant.

So we have a fundamental rule in finance, namely, that one should attempt to match the life of assets with the life of funds supplied to finance those assets. The principle also applied to financing other business areas as well as to capital expenditure. Smaller businesses are inclined to underestimate the amount of long-term finance required for working capital,[16] and to rely too much on overdrafts and delaying payment for goods and services. This happens because of the ease with which short-term finance can be arranged and the lack of formalities. Quite often such money tends to be cheaper as well, because it is at risk for shorter periods.

INTERNAL/EXTERNAL CONSIDERATIONS

Businesses which are operating profitably will be in a position to finance some of their capital-expenditure and working-capital requirements from that surplus. In fact that profit surplus will be supplemented as a source of finance by the amounts a company charges itself for depreciation. Those two sources broadly constitute the internal sources of finance available to companies and represent a very high proportion of the funding of capital expenditure.[17] There is some evidence to suggest that companies use their depreciation provisions for the replacement type of capital expenditure, which must seem a logical allocation.[18] Many companies watch their cash-flow position and its forward projection, and vary their capital expenditure in line with such projections. Such sensitivity is more difficult to achieve in larger companies, but the earlier reference to the Dunlop Rubber Company procedures (pp. 80–1) give some idea how they attempt to achieve such alignment.

Probably there will always be a high proportion of capital expenditure financed from within because such money is the most easily obtained and the purpose for which it is to be used is not subject to the searching analysis of outsiders. In fact, there is some feeling that were such money subject to rather more external control, the quality of capital-expenditure decision-making might improve (see Chapter 3 generally).

It has been suggested that incentives to distribute profit and re-invest via the capital market, rather than retain profits, is a possible mechanism for this,[19] and there has been a minor move in this direction with the imputation system for taxing dividends which removes discrimination in favour of retaining profit.

COST OF CAPITAL CONSIDERATIONS

It has been mentioned earlier that there are various different types of capital available to finance capital expenditure and they each have an annual cost, an interest charge perhaps. Such charges are known as the 'cost of capital' or the 'cost of servicing', and, as we examined in the second section of this chapter, projects for capital expenditure must be able to demonstrate that their prospective return will at least be equal to the cost of capital used. If a variety of sources are used, the project return must equal at least the average of their costs.

The cost of a fixed-interest loan is determined at the time of issue and is designated in its description; 14 per cent Loan Stock 1985 is an example. The company issuing the stock would have to pay 14 per cent p.a. (or, more usually, 7 per cent half-yearly) and repay the whole loan in 1985. Two factors tend to change the simple idea that the cost of our loan is 14 per cent p.a. First, the interest is an allowable charge against corporation tax, and therefore although companies have to pay 14 per cent p.a., they have a compensating tax saving of 14 per cent × the corporation tax rate. Currently, 1975, with corporation tax at 52 per cent that loan would have a net cost of only 0·48 × 14 per cent, that is, approximately 6¾ per cent.

The second complicating factor is that loans are sometimes issued at a lower price than that at which they are repaid by issuing companies. The difference between those two amounts, although not incurred until redemption date, has an equivalent annual cost which can properly be added to the interest burden to arrive at a total annual cost. It must also be remembered that there will be various costs associated with the original issue of the loan, including, the cost of an insurance against it being unsuccessful, known as an 'underwriting commission'.

As we pointed out earlier in Chapter 1, the cost of *preference share capital* is also based on a contractual fixed dividend rate, but because of various tax regulations preference dividends receive relief from income tax, unlike debenture interest which provides relief from corporation tax. Thus, whereas the net cost of debenture interest is the contract rate × (1 − rate of *corporation* tax), the corresponding figure for preference dividends is the contract rate × (1 − rate of *income* tax).

New ordinary shares have no contractual dividend rights attached to them and various attempts have been made to quantify their annual cost. Although owners of such shares have no legal right to a return, they certainly expect something, and if nothing has been forthcoming, it is fairly certain that no further new shares of that kind would be purchased in that company. Hence there is the *expectation* of a return, and usually ordinary shareholders are prepared to receive that return in two different ways. Part of it would be as a dividend each year, and part in the form of a profit when they sell their shares.

In order to provide that return, and therefore preserve the likelihood of being able to sell more ordinary shares in the future, companies must earn in profits from various projects sufficient to pay the annual dividend and ensure an increase in the share price.

The above gives some idea of the constituants of the cost of ordinary capital, and many authorities reduce that to a formula:

$$k = d + g,$$

where k is the cost of ordinary capital, d is the dividend yield currently obtainable on the ordinary shares, and g the expected growth rate in share price and dividends.[20] However, that formula does not seem particularly useful in a practical situation unless one can have a reasonable knowledge of the size of g expected by shareholders, and that is difficult to obtain.

A reasonably manageable approach in practice is that mentioned earlier in this chapter, that is, one of assuming that the total *cost of ordinary shares is the rate which shareholders reasonably expect to receive, and that rate would be somewhat above the return on fixed-interest capital to compensate for the extra risks* inherent in not having a contractual right to a dividend. One normally thinks of a premium of about 3–5 per cent over the return on company long-term loans.

We have already mentioned the substantial extent to which capital expenditure is financed internally through retained profits and depreciation provisions, and we will now discuss their cost to a business.

Retained profits must not be assumed to be cost free merely because companies offer no overt pledge at the time they withhold them. They belong to the risk-taking ordinary shareholders who will expect the company to earn a profit from their use.

It seems unlikely that shareholders distinguish between their original investment and its gradually increasing size provided by retained profits. Indeed, when the shares were purchased there was almost certainly an expectation that the company would retain some profits to provide the wherewithall for an increase in share price. Hence right from the date of purchase there is a link in shareholders' eyes between their share capital and their share of retained earnings.

If that reasoning is accepted, one could conclude that as *shareholders* make no breakdown of their investment into different parts, *they* would have no reason to sub-divide their earnings expectation between that on share capital and that on retained profits. Indeed, financial journals recognise this when they publish data of earnings per share of a company, but no statistics of earnings on retentions.

If we now return to the concept of the cost of ordinary shares, starting from the base that what a company should try to earn is enough to satisfy their owners' expectations, and then link this with the belief that owners' expectations relate to the *total* of their various finances in a company, we will then probably conclude that companies should make no distinction between the cost of ordinary shares and of retained profits. But first something on other views.

Historically our concept has not been very well supported for rather special reasons.[21] The starting point for alternative concepts is that for the retained-profits part of ordinary shareholders' stake, *companies* have an alternative to retention, namely distribution of a dividend. Therefore it is said companies should strive to earn as much on retained profits as shareholders could earn from a re-investment of those profits if they were distributed as a dividend. This is acceptable up to a point, but this concept does not separate *costs* of retained profits from those of the share capital. Presumably ordinary shareholders expect companies to earn as high as could be earned elsewhere on *all* of their stake, not merely the retained earnings. If this was not being achieved, shareholders would take action by selling the *whole of their shareholding* and reinvesting it elsewhere and if such action were on a large scale it would force the ordinary share price of the company downwards. Theoretically directors respond to extended against-an-industry trend of reducing share price by a concerted action to improve profitability on *all* of the ordinary shareholders' stake.

We accept that *a company* may view ordinary share capital and retained profits separately. The former is already sunk in assets and not easily returned to owners, whereas some of the latter may still be liquid and is easily returned. If this distinction is pursued, we come to the second aspect of the concept which in the past has led some observers to conclude that retained earnings have a lower servicing cost than ordinary shares. That second feature was founded on previous tax regulations which first subjected company profits to corporation tax, and then levied income tax if dividends were paid. But the current imputation system no longer involves two lots of taxes on the profits paid as dividends, and only one on profits retained, as was the case with the former regulations. Now, 1975, generally the amount of tax on company earnings is not affected by a distinction between retained profits and distributed profits.

When the former system of company/dividend taxation operated, there was quite a lot of support for the view that if a company could either distribute profits or retain them, then any tax saving resulting from retaining the profits could be used to reduce the earnings requirement on projects financed with the profits not paid out. But since the imputation system has removed the tax advantage to companies of retaining profits, it would also seem to have removed the concession to earning less from projects financed therewith. Hence a former reason for distinguishing between the cost of ordinary capital and retained profits would appear to have been removed.

It seems probable that many who had formerly written of the cheaper cost of retained earnings will agree that the differential in favour of them is no longer so favourable. It remains to be seen whether the identity of costs of ordinary share capital and retained profits becomes more generally accepted, as more is written about it in the environment as influenced by the more modern tax rules.

Before ending the discussion on retained earnings we would point out that the cost of *obtaining* that source is very much less than the cost of obtaining fresh funds from a share issue. We have mentioned already underwriting commission as an expense associated with share issues, but there are also quite substantial professional fees and the necessity when issuing large numbers of shares of doing so at a discount on market price in order to sell the quantity involved. Our comparative discussions in earlier paragraphs have related to the cost of funds obtained, that is, after the deduction of various issuing expenses.

Depreciation provisions have been mentioned as a very large source of long-term finance, and we must now attempt to calculate the cost of servicing them. First, it must be stated that such a source is not cost free. Depreciation provisions belong to somebody, and it seems logical to suggest they belong to the people who provided the *mixture* of funds to purchase assets which are now being depreciated. It is but a short step to suggest that the cost of depreciation provisions is the same as the average cost of the funds which were put together to supply that *mixture;* that is, the cost of depreciation funds is the weighted average of the other long-term funds used by a company.

There is another approach to pricing the depreciation provision source of funds, as indeed there is to all those sources which have no contractual rate. In this case the other approach is to equate the cost of depreciation funds with that of retained profits because the most likely alternative use of both of those sources is the same, namely to pay larger dividends to ordinary shareholders.[22] It is usually agreed that other alternatives are either legally complicated (for example return of share capital) or unlikely (for example return of debentures because they are so much cheaper to service net of tax). One must also add that few senior executives return *capital* to shareholders because to do so reduces the size of the organisation and hence their power, ego, esteem, perks and, probably, salaries. Also, it has connotations of their not knowing what to do with the money, which is not good for their reputations.

Organisations may choose to finance some of their plant via *hire-purchase* facilities. There are advantages in terms of simplicity and of being able to pay for capital expenditure over a period, possibly using the cash flow generated by the plant, and so on. Although a large initial outlay is replaced with smaller regular amounts, that advantage is obtained at no little cost, because hire-purchase finance is usually expensive. Approximately, before tax, it equates to twice the flat rate of interest which is usually mentioned, for example 15 per cent p.a. on original cost works out to approximately 30 per cent p.a. on the amount outstanding.

Leasing is a further method of obtaining the use of assets but avoiding the high initial cost of purchase. Once more, regular amounts have to be paid, and it may also be possible to fund such payments from the annual cash flows of the project. A major difference between leasing and hire purchase is that when using the former the operators never become the owners; ownership remains with the financier. Ownership of assets subject to hire purchase does change from the seller or financial institution to the user.

It is often necessary following a decision to use a particular piece of equipment to have to make another decision, namely should it be purchased or leased. There may be complicating factors to do with maintenance and taxation, but the principles are outlined in the example below (where the complications have been omitted). The procedure is to find the discount rate which reduces the annual lease rentals to a present value equal to the extra cost in the first instance of buying rather than leasing – then to try to borrow money at less than that rate. If one meets with success, it will pay to borrow the money and buy the asset; but, if money can be borrowed only at more than that discount rate, it will pay to lease the asset.

PROBLEM (4)

Should a company buy a machine for £30,000 or lease it for £8000 p.a. for five years *payable in advance*, assuming that a decision has been made that the machine is needed?

The problem can be solved by first finding the interest rate which supplies the set of discount factors which reduce the leasing rents to the same sum as the purchase price of £30,000.

SOLUTION TO PROBLEM (4)

(a) Year	(b) Rent (£000)	(c) Try 20 per cent	(bc)	(d) Try 17 per cent	(bd)
0	8	1·0	8000	1·0	8000
1	8	0·833	6664	0·855	6840
2	8	0·694	5552	0·731	5848
3	8	0·579	4632	0·624	4992
4	8	0·482	3856	0·534	4272
			28704		29952[23]
	∴ 20 per cent is too high			∴ 17 per cent is about right	

The conclusion to this simplified problem is that the cost of leasing finance is 17 per cent p.a., and if money can be borrowed at less than that, then other things being equal the asset should be purchased.

The Concept of Average Cost of Capital

We have discussed the concept of quantifying costs of different kinds of capital because one of the basic questions which tends to be asked of any proposed investment is: 'Will it earn at least as much as the interest rate on money used to finance it?' But it is unusual for companies to allocate particular sources of finance to particular projects. It is more usual to treat all of the sources as an amalgamated fund and to draw from that total for each project. Projects then would have to earn at least as much as the average cost of the sources in that total. It is likely that the total fund will be made up of unequal proportions of various types of finance, and therefore we do not require a simple average of their costs, but an average weighted in the same proportions as the sums of capital supplied, for example the weighted average of £100,000 (annual cost 10 per cent) and £200,000 (annual cost 20 per cent) would be 16⅔ per cent:

$$£100,000 \text{ p.a. at 10 per cent costs} \quad £10,000$$
$$£200,000 \text{ p.a. at 20 per cent costs} \quad £40,000$$

$$£300,000 \text{ p.a.} \qquad \text{costs} \quad £50,000 \text{ i.e. } 16⅔ \text{ per cent}$$

Financing the Operation of Plant and Equipment

We will proceed in this section to examine financing of operations which follow from making use of the equipment purchased with the capital expenditure which we examined earlier. Initially we will look at the sequence of these operations, followed by a discussion of why they need to be financed and then explain the sources which are utilised.

Each type of industry will have certain specialist features but a general model can be envisaged which has the following stages:

(1) Obtaining work;
(2) Obtaining materials;
(3) Conversion of materials, often using capital equipment;
(4) Sometimes stocking whilst awaiting sale;
(5) Sale and the allowance of a credit period; and
(6) Payment by customer and receipt by producer.

It will be appreciated that the cycle of events outlined could involve a considerable time scale. The time would be measured in years for some big construction work, and maybe days for some small repetitive manufacturers. The customer may not contribute any finance for months, but during that period payments will have to be made for wages, some overheads and possibly the materials. This part of our book is concerned with how businesses obtain the ability to pay those wages etc. before the fruits of the labour have been paid by the customer. Financing material purchases can take a variety of forms, but almost certainly the first form used will be *trade credit;* that is, just not paying 'yet awhile' for the goods bought. Suppliers recognise this as accepted practice and they use the giving of trade credit to their commercial advantage in a number of ways, for customers may choose suppliers on the basis of credit given as well as price, quality, and so on. Also, suppliers may want to have an even rate of production during periods of fluctuating, particularly seasonal demand. In such cases, in periods of low sales they quickly become congested with stock produced but not sold, and one way of overcoming the problem is to encourage their customers to take stock into their premises, but not to pay for it until after it is·used.

The cost of trade credit to users of materials occurs when payment is withheld until after the lapse of any cash-discount period. A close approximation to its costs then can be obtained by solving the equation:

$$I = \frac{365}{CT_d - CA_d} \times \%DO$$

where I = cost of trade discount, CT_d = credit taken in days, CA_d = credit allowed in days by discount terms, and $\%DO$ = percentage cash discount offered.

This source of credit/finance is easy to obtain, extensively used and generally rather expensive. In 1959 the Radcliffe Committee stated that at the time of its report the amount of trade credit outstanding in this country between industrial and commercial companies whose shares were quoted on the Stock Exchange amounted to more than the total credit extended by the clearing banks.

The next stage in an organisation's business cycle is to convert materials into goods that can be sold. That stage incurs considerable expense in terms of wages and overheads such as electricity, rates and many others. It is likely that a variety of sources of finance will be used to pay for those expenses, and of considerable importance is a part of the fund of long-term capital discussed earlier. It is often overlooked that the requirement to finance these expenses until receipts come in from goods sold is a permanent requirement, and is therefore long term and, prudently, should be covered to a considerable extent with long-term money. What often happens is that some of that requirement will be financed by a form of *bank credit*. Bank credit can take various forms but for the situation described it is likely to be an overdraft facility. The cost of this will be related to the bank's base rate, and anything up to about 4 per cent above that figure may be quoted. Additionally, the bank may charge a commitment commission, which is an annual sum for committing the bank's resources for the organisation's benefit. Bank credit is relatively cheap and there is a thankful absence of time-consuming administration. Bank managers sometimes ask to see forward estimates of cash flows so that they may have some reassurance of repayment, and incidentally for future use when judging the organisation's ability to predict its future. Sometimes bank managers will ask for security for the credit they provide.

Banks are also traditionally used to finance holdings of stock and the credit periods taken by customers. There are various ways in which they provide help with customer finance. In addition to overdrafts they are also involved, either directly or through subsidiary or associated companies, with *discounting invoices, bills of exchange and promissory notes*. The principle of all of these procedures is the same, namely that the bank will advance all or some of the debt mentioned on the document concerned in return for an interest charge for the period between the due date and the date of advance/discount. There are numerous variations of procedure in practice, some of which involve improvement of the credit rating of the persons named in the invoice or bill of exchange etc., by adding the additional name of an organisation of maximum creditworthiness such as a merchant bank.

Further Reading

Tibar Barna, *Investment and Growth Policies in British Industrial Firms*, National Institute of Economic and Social Research (Cambridge University Press, 1962).

Ronald Edwards and Harry Townsend, *Business Enterprise. Its Growth and Organisation* (London: Macmillan, 1961).

I. Fisher, *The Theory of Interest* (New York: Macmillan, 1930).

Robert Jones and Oliver Marriott, *Anatomy of a Merger* (London: Pan Books, 1970).

A. J. Merrett and Allen Sykes, *Capital Budgeting and Company Finance* (London: Longmans, 1966).

K. Midgley and R. G. Burns, *Business Finance and the Capital Market*, 2nd edn (London: Macmillan, 1972).

Peter Readman, *The European Money Puzzle* (London: Michael Joseph, 1973).

Alex Rubner, *The Ensnared Shareholder* (London: Macmillan, 1965).

J. M. Samuels and F. M. Wilkes, *Management of Company Finance* (London: Nelson, 1971).

Alfred P. Sloan Jr, *My Years with General Motors* (London: Pan Piper, 1965).

Bruce R. Williams and W. P. Scott, *Investment Proposals and Decisions* (London: Allen & Unwin, 1965).

'Public Sector Investment, Economic or Political Decisions, *Barclays Review* (August 1974).

'Accounting for Society. Cost Benefit Analysis', *Barclays Review* (August 1974).

Nationalised Industries. A review of Financial and Economic Objectives, Cmnd. 3437 (London: H.M.S.O., 1967).

British Steel Corporation: 10 Year Development Strategy, Cmnd. 5226 (London: H.M.S.O., 1973).

H. H. Scholefield, N. S. McBain and J. Bagwell, 'The Effects of Inflation on Investment Appraisal', *Journal of Business Finance* (Summer 1973).

CHAPTER 5

The Markets: Procedures and Control

The City of London is an important market-place for many commodities, including money – hence its role as an international financial centre. There are several related financial markets. The capital market is usually described as that dealing in longer-term funds, and the money market in shorter-term funds.

It is common practice nowadays to refer to two divisions of the money market, namely the classical markets and the parallel markets. The former deals in Treasury bills (short-term loans to the government – a ninety-day life is common), local authority bills, short-dated gilts (loans to the government of up to five years' duration) and commercial bills. Commercial bills are acknowledgements of debts which can be sold (discounted). They are drawn by commercial companies and accepted by either other commercial companies (trade bills) or banks (bank bills). The parallel markets deal in finance house deposits, local authority deposits, euro-currency deposits, certificates of deposit, inter-company and inter-bank deposits.[1]

There are many institutions involved with the capital and money markets but the two which dominate those two markets are respectively the Stock Exchange and the clearing banks. The bulk of this book is directed to examining the capital market, but before moving towards that we should re-emphasise that the banking system is enormously important. For some periods during the early 1970s when some sources of new long-term capital had almost dried up, U.K. industry was increasingly supported by the banking system. London is the centre of the U.K. banking system, and also pays host to the world's bankers. For example, there are more U.S. banks represented in London than in New York, and large numbers of banks from Europe, and over twenty from Japan, also do business in the City,[2] much of it on an international scale.

The clearing banks have changed and developed considerably since the early 1960s. As mentioned previously, there have been mergers between the clearing banks, and with merchant banks; also, expansion into leasing, factoring, hire purchase and medium-term loans as means of providing alternative forms of finance. Customer services have been improved with the provision of insurance broking, credit cards and unit trusts, and there is now more meaningful profit information in the banks' published accounts.

But all of these innovations have not enabled the banks to escape criticism, which includes the not unusual claim that large, long-established institutions are too inbred. Too few graduates, too many gentlemen amateurs in the board rooms, years of specialisation in short-term finance, which has sired a confinement to short-term decisions, an absence of enthusiasm about using the rigorous control systems and analytical techniques used by the American banks, and the lack of status afforded to non-banking specialists, are all comments that have been documented.[3]

Notwithstanding the above comments, the clearing banks must be credited with the channelling of large amounts of surplus short-term funds and bank credit to industry. Undoubtedly large sums have been provided for the purchase of new equipment as well as the more normal provision of working capital; and, at times, there have been many employees of local industry who have a local bank manager to thank for the maintenance of their job.

The Stock Exchange

The Stock Exchange is the prime institution in the stock market or capital market, and it is a specialist market place. The London Stock Exchange is merely one of London's specialist markets, and others include Smithfields, Covent Garden, Billingsgate and the Baltic Exchange. The London Stock Exchange originated in the seventeenth century from informal gatherings of dealers in stocks and shares in the coffee houses around the Royal Exchange, and it has not moved far away.

Discussions on the functions and attributes of the Stock Exchange and the capital market often become emotive. The main function of any stock exchange is to provide the mechanism for the exchange of shares which already exist. This so-called 'secondary market' provides a service which, it is traditionally argued, must be present before any issues of additional shares and stock by industry or government will be taken up, and hence funds provided for new projects, and so on. The idea is that investors must have the facility for selling-out should the need arise.

Criticisms of the Stock Exchange and capital market are often that it concentrates too much on the exchange aspect and not enough on the capital-raising. A television interview on the morning following one of the general elections in the early 1970s provided an excellent example of such a criticism. A well-known trade-union leader made an unexpected comment about not wanting to break up the present capitalist system, but he wanted to see it providing some *risk* capital, and being prepared to take *risks*. Presumably he was worried about a shortage of funds for employment-providing projects. A very good answer could have been a comment read some months later:

> that even the best machinery for raising capital – and no-one would wish to claim that ours, excellent though it is, might not in some ways be improved – cannot function in a climate where inflation and uncertainty make it unattractive for savers to lend money to industry on any terms which industry could conceivably afford to pay.[4]

The principal participants in the Stock Exchange can be easily identified from an imaginary purchase of 100 ordinary shares in Speedy Ferries Limited. This rather modest purchase may be started by a telephone call to one's bank identifying the shares and the maximum price to be paid, say 60p each. The bank then contacts a stockbroker who will be a member of the Stock Exchange.

Stockbrokers are agents whose job is to effect their customers' instructions on the best terms possible. They are remunerated by a commission, the minimum rates of which are fixed by the Stock Exchange, of which they are members. Our stockbroker will approach one or more specialist dealers in Speedy Ferries' shares, and ask for a price. The dealer, known as a 'jobber', will quote two prices – one at which he will buy and the other his selling price for the shares. He should quote these two prices without asking whether he is required to buy or sell. The stockbroker should place the order with the jobber, quoting the best price for the ultimate customer. Jobbers are remunerated by selling at higher prices than those at which they buy.

There are variations in practice for larger deals. For example, the broker may attempt to directly match buy and sell orders in the same shares emanating from his clients. Also, for large transactions the jobber will require to be informed whether an enquiry is for a purchase or a sale. There are three major criticisms of the transaction system mentioned.

(a) Minimum scales may tend to benefit stockbrokers more than their clients. There are many who think that more commission and price competition is required, and that these stalwarts of *laissez-faire* should be subject to its rigours as well as its benefits.

(b) The duplication of expenses to clients by having two stages to go through, namely both broker and jobber. Is this another case of overmanning in a British enterprise, because such a system does not exist elsewhere?

(c) Small companies do not receive the same attention from the present jobbing system as is afforded the larger companies. One recommendation is that there should be a separately organised specialist market-place for smaller companies.[5]

Stockbrokers have greatly increased their services to customers in the field of research and investment advice. Usually such services are treated as an overhead by the brokers and not charged for separately. The quality of the advice is difficult to measure because of the difficulty of isolating all the variables, and there is no published comparison known to the authors of the standards of investment advice offered by different stockbroking firms.[6]

The Stock Exchange itself has recently moved into modern premises which is perhaps the most obvious of a number of changes since the 1960s in the stock market. The number of stockbroking and jobbing firms have concentrated into fewer, larger units. Part of the reason has been to share the high costs of computerisation and additional research. Provincial and foreign branch offices have been opened, and limited partnerships permitted, the latter move being made to facilitate additional sources of finance to be tapped from people and companies who are prepared to forgo day-to-day management in return for limited liability.

More data are now provided in respect of turnover in addition to such things as details of *some* bargains, interest and dividends on individual securities, and the wealth of information in the *Stock*

Exchange Year Book. The Exchange itself has computerised some of its administrative procedures, and advertising by members firms of their services is now permitted.

The Stock Exchange requirements which companies must observe in order to have their securities quoted are overhauled periodically, and generally are more demanding than what is required by company law. Examples of this have included provision of data on groups of companies, breakdown of trading results where a company or group carries on widely different operations, and the publication of half-yearly results. Importantly, there is also a compensation fund to safeguard the public, should a member go bankrupt.

All these changes have occurred but there are still many calls for further improvements over quite a wide range of activities, some of which have already been mentioned. Other criticisms include the following.

(*a*) Jobbers have reduced competition between themselves by operating jointly in given securities, and this in turn has reduced the number of different prices available to brokers. Also, margins between buying and selling prices have widened to the benefit of jobbers and the detriment of other investors.

(*b*) Sanctions against quoted companies and members are rare. The only possibility in the former case is to suspend the company's quotation, which seems to harm the very people it is seeking to protect, shareholders, rather than the offenders. (In some cases these will overlap in part, namely where offending officers are major shareholders.) Although suspensions and expulsion of existing members are rare, there has been increased control on new membership since the requirement that all new members must have passed Stock Exchange examinations.

(*c*) The Stock Exchange is too secretive about its own affairs, particularly concerning jobbers. There is also the criticism of it being too traditional, but one must beware of too speedily condemning proven, albeit traditional, methods. The trouble is that too often the secrecy prevents confirmation of efficiency as well as hiding the reverse.

(*d*) More innovation is required on the grading of fixed-interest stocks so that the differences between high-class issues and lower ones are brought out.

(*e*) Members should re-accustom some of their clients to investing longer term for a return, and away from the speculative fever which has been prevalent for too long.

Perhaps the most significant development in the stock market in recent years has been the formalised bypassing of part of the Stock Exchange system by the introduction of ARIEL. This is a computerised block trading system jointly owned by the members of the Accepting House Committee (certain major merchant banks who have large, often very large, investment management departments). The system is designed wherever possible to match the security transactions of its subscribers, who in turn are many of the larger financial institutions. Such a system will be cheaper for members because of the elimination of the jobber's margin, and lower commission rates.

The New Issue Market

The new issue (or primary) market is that section of the stock market concerned with the expansion of shares and stock available to the public. Most of these shares are new shares, the sales proceeds of which go to companies to finance expansion, modernisation, and so on, that is, to generate new tangible assets and working capital. There are also two categories of new issue which do not have this function. First, there are issues by investment companies who merely reinvest the proceeds of their new issue in the purchase of other companies' existing shares. Second, there is the issue by smaller companies of shares already in existence, but owned by the controlling shareholder and his family. Such issues may be to release the owner's capital which is tied up in physical assets rather than a more easily spendable commodity. This practice is probably necessary before the new issue market can be used to increase the funds available to the *companies* concerned.

Hence the new issue market does not always involve new shares, and not all capital raised there goes to purchase new hardware or to finance increases in production activities.

There are a number of specialists involved with new issues. Issuing houses (many of whom are merchant banks) and stockbrokers organise and administer much of the issue. They will ensure that Stock Exchange and legal requirements are fulfilled and will advise on the type of security to be issued, the method of issue and the security's initial selling price. Success of the issue, in terms of all the shares offered being ultimately purchased, is guaranteed with the help of underwriters. These are a large cross-section of financial institutions, for example life assurance companies, pension funds, investment trusts and various organisations and individuals whose investment affairs are managed by merchant banks and others on underwriting lists. Those underwriters will guarantee the issue for a commission, and will also have a considerable influence on the issue price because fairly obviously they will not insure an issue which is considered to be overpriced for the volume of shares involved.

The clearing banks often also become involved by providing the services of their new issue and registrar departments. The administration for a large new issue can be enormous in view of the work entailed, with large quantities of cheques, new issue documents and ultimately share certificates. The specialist services of solicitors and accountants are also required.

Factors determining the type of security chosen for issue were outlined in Chapter 1, and the variety of methods of issue are mentioned below.

For the established company with an existing Stock Exchange quotation, one of two methods of issue is usually chosen. If new ordinary shares are being sold, they are usually offered first to existing shareholders in proportion to their current holdings; that is to say, existing supporters of the company have the first opportunity to buy more shares. Such issues are known as *rights issues*, and are priced below the current market price because more shares will be on offer than in the normal supply situation when current market prices are made.

If the established company is issuing debenture or loan stock, the common practice is for the advisers to the issue (issuing house/merchant bank) to place the shares with clients and contacts. This procedure is used because loan stock is normally held by the financial institutions, that is, a limited market. Such issues are known as *placings*.

Smaller companies may also have new issues of ordinary shares placed with institutions if it is thought that the issue is too small or the company too unknown yet to attract support from the public at large. Points in favour of placings include certain cost savings, notably the underwriting commission. There are also significant savings in printing, postage and document handling charges because large numbers of people are not involved.

When it is thought that a share issue by a company new to the Stock Exchange will be a success, the issue is often via *an offer for sale*. This involves the issuing house first buying all the shares being offered for sale, and then advertising and arranging their sale to the general public at a somewhat higher price. Note that there is no large existing body of shareholders to whom the sale can first be offered. Very occasionally a variant of the above, known as *an offer for sale by tender*, is used whereby the public is invited to tender a price for the shares being offered, and the shares will be allocated at the single highest price at which all the shares could be disposed of, and a sufficiently large number of shareholders created to enable a broad market to be obtained.

Critics of the new issue market point to the small amounts of risk capital raised (see, for example, Table 2.1, p. 24, and Chapter 3). They suggest that it is merely an appendage to the main activity of making profits from short-term dealing (speculating in the Stock Exchange by members of the market menagerie: bulls (who hope for rising prices), bears (who hope for falling prices) and stags (who hope for rising prices of new issues)). It is perhaps interesting to establish what degree of emphasis is directed to the issue of new risk capital rather than the exchange of existing equities. A broad indication is given in Table 5.1 where the net issue of ordinary shares is compared with London Stock Exchange turnover in equities, and it emphasises the small part in Stock Exchange transactions which is attributable to capital-raising new issues.[7]

If the new issue market does not provide a great deal of new capital, there must be an explanation, and one would imagine it cannot be because the City discourages these issues. After all, why discourage something on which one sector can earn high issuing fees, and of course another sector, the jobbers and brokers, at a later point can earn commissions from the exchange of these new shares? The answer seems more likely to reflect the reluctance of industry and commerce to use the new issue market. There are several reasons for considering alternative sources of finances, but one can readily see that retained profits and depreciation provisions are least troublesome to draw upon. There are no administration costs, no rules and regulations to observe, and no need to publish

Table 5.1

Stock market activity

	(a) London Stock Exchange turnover in equities (£m.)	(b) Net issues of ordinary shares (£m.)	(b) as percentage of (a)
1966	3600	124	3·4
1967	5800	65	1·1
1968	9100	299	3·3
1969	8700	177	2·0
1970	8800	39	0·4
1971	13400	152	1·1
1972	20000	317	1·6
1973	17000	98	0·6

Sources: Column (a) *Moorgate and Wall Street Review* (Spring 1974) p. 16; column (b) *Barclays Review* (August 1974).

detailed information which could attract criticism. On the other hand, the procedures associated with a new issue attract large fees which are not associated with internal sources of funds.

There has been much adverse comment about costs of a new issue, particularly when account is taken of the difference between the price the company gets for its shares newly issued and the frequently much higher price at which newly issued shares are dealt in when dealings commence.[8] Although the financial press talks of a successful issue as one in which all the new shares are sold, from the company's viewpoint a successful equity issue is one which brings in most money for least shares, with minimum costs. From the stock market members' and speculators' point of view, a successful issue might be thought to be one where the fees, commissions and dealing profits are greatest. A compromise may have to be reached for both groups to want to become involved, and perhaps industry's view is that stock market new issue services are overpriced, with the result that they are used sparingly. Reassurances from issuing houses that new issues must be keenly priced to encourage support and a large market may not cut much ice with industrialists. The large market and keen price may benefit certain market operators but not, at least initially, the company's capital-expenditure programmes.

Another criticism of the new issue market is that it is too tied to current share prices. When share prices are high, and hence new issues are attractive to companies, it is likely to be because recent profits earned and short-term profit prospects are high. At such times companies' internal cash flow is likely to be either high or, at any rate, on the upgrade. In such cases recourse to the new issue market may be unnecessary from the point of view of immediate need for capital expenditure, because what funds are not contributed internally could very likely be made available by banks. Equity issues are nevertheless very popular at such times, as they raise the equity base and lower the gearing ratio so the company is well placed for borrowing at some future time. The converse also applies. When companies need outside funds their share price may well be low, and therefore a share issue may be unattractive to investors and to the company. Such a phenomenon may at least in part be the cause of direct government action in the supply of business capital.

Regulation and Control

Perhaps the most effective form of regulation and/or protection within the capital market is to be found in the degree of competition prevailing there. If this were perfect in every respect, then, apart from the need to counter fraud and deception, there need be little or no further control by way of rules or legislation. Unfortunately, there are some aspects of the market which mar any theoretical image of perfection; hence the need for certain requirements to be observed by the participants. However, another reason for the network of controls relating to the capital market is the complex nature of the product. In the market for apples the product is fairly well understood by those dealing and there is little need for consumer protection. Such simplicity is not so evident in the market for a rather more complex or sophisticated commodity or service, say foreign holidays. In the market for securities the commodity is neither simple, easily evaluated nor fully open to inspection in many respects.

A perfect market has four principle characteristics: homogeneity of commodity; a large number of suppliers, none of which is sufficiently large to influence price; full knowledge of conditions within the market by all participants; and freedom of entry into the market. The Stock Market falls short of these criteria in that the suppliers of particular securities and the securities themselves *within certain classes* are not abundant, free entry does not exist and certainly the degree of knowledge prevailing amongst participants is much less than optimum.

Legislation, control and regulation can offset some of these imperfections and also do much to counter fraud, deception and improper use of inside information. Very broadly, the framework of control aims to ensure that information is adequate, clearly presented and readily available to all, that the participants in the market behave honestly, openly and fairly, and that special advantages are not enjoyed by a favoured few. Even an outline of the regulatory machinery must of necessity be sketchy within the confines of this small book, but sufficient can be said to indicate the approach adopted and some of the problems of achieving a successful balance of control and flexibility.

The principal legislation governing the capital market is to be found in the Companies Acts and the Prevention of Frauds (Investments) Act. The Companies Acts are designed to ensure adequate disclosure of facts and of personal interests, to provide a means of control by equity-holders, to clarify certain obligations of directors and others, and to regulate such matters as incorporation and winding up. The Prevention of Fraud (Investments) Act of 1958 regulates the licensing exemption and conduct of dealers in securities and, particularly, the manner in which circulars from dealers may be used.[9] The primary authority for such supervision rests with the Department of Trade, the main instrument of intervention being the appointment of inspectors under Sections 164–5 and 334 of the 1948 Companies Act. The Board of Trade may also call for the production of books and papers by authority of Sections 109–18 of the 1967 Companies Act. The appointment of inspectors has not been frequently used as an instrument of control. Thus during the period 1950–66 there were an average of four appointments per year, but this must be seen against an average of about ninety applications each year. Few large companies have been subjected to inspection, probably the best known instances in recent years being those involving Pergamon and Lonrho. Such investigations may take two years or more, and thus can hardly be regarded as providing a prompt remedy, although the existence of this sanction may act as a deterrent to potential transgressors of the written and unwritten code of good market behaviour. If transgressions amount to fraud or breach of statutory provisions, action against a company may be taken privately by individuals or by the Director of Public Prosecutions. A private action could be very expensive and evidence difficult to accumulate, and hence this is rarely undertaken against quoted companies.

Much of the regulation of the capital market, however, is on an extra-legal or voluntary basis. Stock Exchange Rules and Regulations apply principally to members, but as the latter act on behalf of the public 'subject to the Rules and Regulations of the Stock Exchange', the public by inference are also bound. The Stock Exchange Council has power to reprimand, suspend or expel members where circumstances warrant such penalties, and there are rules against market rigging or creation of a false market. Before granting a quotation it can subject companies to rigorous examination. Appendix 34 to the Rules, in setting standards for prospectus documents, goes beyond the requirements of Schedule 4 of the 1948 Companies Act in requiring much greater disclosure on such matters as directors' interests, details of indebtedness at the latest possible date, and statements on financial and trading prospects. Requirements for listing also contain obligations to be accepted by the issuer to maintain proper standards for the future which also exceed in rigour certain corresponding requirements of current company legislation. Failure of a company to honour the undertaking may be countered by the suspension of its quotation. Unfortunately, as mentioned earlier, this sanction may damage shareholders more than the company officers responsible and is used rarely as a disciplinary measure against quoted companies. It can be used to good effect, however, during the currency of a takeover bid (at the request of the Panel on Takeovers and Mergers) to prevent dealing in the absence of adequate information or clarification of an obscure situation.

In order to protect the financial interests of investors, the Stock Exchange Council maintains strict control over the financial affairs of its member-firms and, as a further protection, a discretionary compensation fund can be drawn upon to meet claims from the public arising from losses relating to transactions through a defaulting member.

While it is true to say that the effect of these measures has been that misconduct, discrimination and avoidable financial loss have been kept to low levels, there have been, and probably will continue to be, cases of improper private gain. The occasion of a takeover bid, especially, has provided many instances of questionable behaviour in the past. The major abuses which affect shareholders in takeovers can be summarised as those arising from lack of adequate disclosure, from dealings which discriminate between different groups of shareholders, and from misuse of powers by directors or controlling shareholders. The tensions which can arise are not very difficult to understand: the bidder will aim to gain control of the 'offeree' company as cheaply as possible; the managers of the offeree company are likely to be considering the effect of the bid on their own careers, income and wealth; shareholders will be looking for the best offer and no less favourable treatment than their fellows; and employees will be anxious about their future employments and prospects. Censurable behaviour in the past has included the following: directors of the offeree company favouring one of rival bidders to the detriment of shareholders' interests; directors fighting off a bid by making misleadingly optimistic forecasts as to future profits; unequal treatment for shareholders, for example institutional shareholders being favoured; and bidders acquiring shares in a potential victim company in a stealthy and underhand manner.[10]

The inadequacy of existing legislation and control to deal with fast-developing situations and behaviour (amounting to a breach of principles of fair dealing, while not actually in breach of the law or any regulation), led to the formulation of the City Code, which emerged from a set of rules originally drawn up in 1959 by a City working party. It represents a self-regulating procedure by the City to ensure fair dealing during takeovers by the provision of a set of *principles* of conduct to be observed in bid situations, and fairly detailed *rules* subject to practice notes and revision as necessary. There are at present twelve general principles and thirty-nine rules expressed in the Code. It is emphasised that the spirit as well as the precise wording of the Code must be observed. A main theme of the principles is that boards and their advisers have a primary duty to act in the best interests of shareholders and to ensure that they have the necessary information to enable them to assess their position and have time to make a decision; but these interests are to be considered *together with* those of employees and creditors. The rules give guidance on the correct approach to be adopted at different stages of the bid: for example details as to whom an offer should be made; the degree of secrecy and extent of disclosure; the correct procedure to be adopted by boards of directors; and so on.

The leading financial institutions of the City are represented on the Panel which administers the Code. The Panel has a permanent secretariat which monitors all relevant documents relating to take-overs. It has an independent chairman and vice-chairman nominated by the Governor of the Bank of England. It is prepared to offer advice at any stage of merger transactions; it reserves the right to be consulted in cases of doubt as to interpretation of its rules; and there is a right to appeal from its rulings to a committee headed by a Lord Justice of Appeal. The Code and Panel thus provide a basis of a system of voluntary self-discipline. The sanctions which can be engineered by the Panel, supported as it is by, among other bodies, the Stock Exchange Council, the Issuing Houses Association, the Department of Trade and Industry, the Accepting Houses Committee, the Association of Investment Trusts, the British Insurance Association, the Committee of London Clearing Bankers and the National Association of Pension Funds, include the suspension of the quotation of a company's shares, the withdrawal of a licensed dealer's exemption, expulsion of a member of the Stock Exchange, the institution of a statutory enquiry, and, against individuals, public reprobation, for example a statement that a particular person is unfit to be a director of a public company.

A cardinal merit of self-regulation in the management and supervision of the capital market is the degree of flexibility and speed in meeting new situations. Although the Panel has not the wider powers and backing of law available to the U.S. Securities and Exchange Commission (S.E.C.), it can take action to defeat those who would otherwise operate within the margin of law but outside the bounds of fair play. Because it has been fostered by the City, it is thought to be more likely to be respected by City institutions than a regulatory system which is imposed. By comparison with the S.E.C. it is exceedingly cheap in operation, and, as it allows reasonable freedom of operation, it encourages rather than repels international business.

The system has, however, been subject to quite severe criticism. As a body which has to make judgements on important issues, the Panel suffers the disadvantages that it cannot subpoena witnesses, take evidence on oath or require the production of documents. It also lacks protection against actions for defamation.

The Panel is the sole interpreter of the City Code: it acts as both prosecutor and judge, and denies defendants the right to engage counsel. It faces difficulties in exerting pressure on persons outside City institutions; its small staff and the limited scope of its powers may not provide a sufficient deterrent or enable it to effectively monitor all situations and documentation relating to takeover bids; and it has been slow to take the initiative in respect of certain abuses such as insider trading and warehousing (that is, 'takeover by stealth'). In general, there is the overriding difficulty of persuading the public that it is right for the market authorities to be judge in their own cause.

There are other aspects of the market for capital which are also subject to some degree of self-regulation, and as these areas overlap somewhat there tends to be some confusion as to exactly where authority lies. For example, the Companies Acts require public companies to publish considerable detail of their affairs in their annual reports. The Stock Exchange General Undertaking may require additional and/or more frequent information; and, to add to the complex of authority, the Accounting Standards Steering Committee may have prepared Statements of Standard Accounting Practice which it requires members of the major accounting bodies to observe. These are meant to be clear-cut principles which, when applied to financial accounts, give an objectively true and fair view of the financial position – and profit or loss. They have covered a number of accounting topics, including, for example, earnings per share, inflation accounting, treatment of taxation in accounts, and sources and applications of funds. An instance of the confusion of authority which may occur arose when the Sandilands Committee, appointed by the government, made recommendations on inflation accounting which differed radically from those contained in the (provisional) Accounting Standard.

Some critics consider that the weakest aspect of the present system of regulation is that 'whole areas of control and professional conduct are subject to the vagaries, not of state law, but of various sections of private enterprise'.[11] Bodies such as the Takeover Panel, the Stock Exchange Council, the Accounting Standards Steering Committee, trade and professional associations, and Protection Committees of the Institutional Investors may exert influence or exercise authority over types of market activity which may be also subject to official control by government departments or statutorily established agencies. The extra-legal authorities provide only limited protection for investors in the market and their sanctions may not be sufficiently rigorous. Whether the various shortcomings of the self-regulatory complex are sufficiently serious to justify the establishment of new machinery such as the Companies Commission, suggested by the 1974 Labour Party Green Paper,[12] which would supervise and co-ordinate many aspects of market regulation relating to company securities, or whether the virtues of flexibility, self-assent and economy more than offset the imperfections of the existing system, will no doubt be settled in forthcoming company legislation.

Further Reading

R. J. Briston, *The Stock Exchange and Investment Analysis* (London: Allen & Unwin, 1975) chs. 1, 3, 4.

K. Midgley, *Companies and their Shareholders – the Uneasy Relationship* (Institute of Chartered Secretaries and Administrators, 1975).

Jack Revell, *Changes in British Banking – the Growth of a Secondary Banking System* Hill, Samuel Occasional Paper No. 3 (1968).

E. Stamp and C. Marley, *Accounting Principles and the City Code* (London: Butterworth, 1970).

Richard Spiegelberg, *The City – Power Without Accountability* (London: Blond & Briggs, 1973).

City Capital Markets Committee, *Supervision of the Securities Market*, Answers to questions contained in the Inquiry of the Department of Trade (June 1974).

Labour Party Green Paper, *The Community and the Company*, Working Group of the Labour Party Industrial Policy Sub-Committee (1974).

'London Money Markets', *Barclays Review* (November 1972).

'The Eurocurrency Markets', *Barclays Review* (February 1976).

P. K. Woolley, 'The Economics of the U.K. Stock Exchange', *Moorgate and Wall Street Review* (Spring 1974).

CHAPTER 6

Conclusion: the Effectiveness of the U.K. Capital Market

Assessments of the effectiveness of any part of the economic mechanism of the United Kingdom tend these days to be related to the disappointing post-war growth record of the U.K. economy in comparison with those of many other industrial nations. Whether the object of study is labour relations, monopoly and mergers, or the capital market, an important issue in the mind of the investigator is: to what extent are any imperfections in the operating mechanism responsible for the poor performance of the economy? There are of course various ways of measuring the success of an economy, but if measured in terms of growth of real gross national product per annum, the United Kingdom's recent performance can be compared (see Table 6.1).

Table 6.1
Percentage growth of real G.N.P.

	Average 1959–60 to 1972–3	1974	1975*	1976*
United Kingdom	3·3	0·1	−2·25	0
France	5·9	3·9	−2	3
West Germany	4·9	0·4	−3·75	3·25
Italy	5·6	3·2	−4·5	1·5
Japan	10·9	−1·8	1·25	4·25
United States	4·2	−2·1	−3·0	5·75

* Forecast.
Source: O.E.C.D., *Economic Outlook*.

Factors Affecting Investment and Growth

A factor which has an important bearing on growth of national income is the level of investment and the composition of that investment. (Another important factor relating to growth in the United Kingdom is the level of exports which can be achieved, for any shortcomings in this respect may indirectly constrain imports of raw materials necessary for growth.) The levels of capital investment per head in real terms in this country has advanced very slowly during the past decade; indeed in 1975 in manufacturing industry it was less than the level achieved in the late 1960s and was well below the rate of that in France and West Germany (see Table 2.4). It is therefore relevant to ask whether the organisation of the U.K. capital market, and attitudes within it, can be in any way responsible for the country's very modest economic performance. Certainly some pronouncements from government and trade-union sources have appeared to suggest that this is so, the general tenor of the argument being that because there has been a tendency for funds to be directed into property investment or areas where there are prospects of short-term capital gains, insufficient funds are made available for long-term investment, which, although not offering attractive short-term prospects, would nevertheless be worthwhile and beneficial to the country's economy. In a similar vein it has been argued that financial intermediaries 'that are responsible for channelling available funds into companies have not been prepared to invest long-term in British industry' and that this has meant that U.K. industry has needed to invest for short-term profits and 'that the cost of capital to companies in the U.K. has been higher than the cost of capital to companies in other countries'.[1] The inference that 'the capital market in the U.K. does not seem in recent years to have been over-successful in allocating funds into the more desirable, the more productive investment opportunities'[2] must now be examined. (Many detailed critical observations have already been made in earlier chapters. See, for example, Chapter 2 for some international comparisons and Chapter 5 for comments on the clearing banks and the Stock Exchange. Chapter 4 also makes the point that industry's allocation of funds received has often been made with an alarming lack of objectivity.)

An initial observation is that there has in fact been no shortage of capital or lack of support during recent years for capital projects which have been identified by private and institutional investors as offering prospects of an adequate return. However, this depends for its validity on the definition of 'adequate'. It may not answer the challenge that investors have been less than fully prepared to look to the long term for that adequacy. On the other hand, as investors rightfully expect to secure for themselves, or for those on whose behalf they act, a sufficient recompense for their outlay, capital will not be supplied at unrealistically low rates. As pointed out in Chapter 1, the rate of inflation (that is, the loss in value of the currency) is reflected in the terms at which investors are prepared to make funds available. As rates of inflation during the 1970s had risen from 5 per cent in 1970 to 25 per cent in 1975, it is hardly surprising that the cost of capital became *prima facie* prohibitive for many companies. As it is, investors have supplied capital at rates which gave a negative return; for example, an interest rate of 15 per cent before income tax, and with inflation per annum at 25 per cent the standard-taxpaying investor is left −15 per cent worse off after tax! Although lenders have thus suffered losses, they naturally look for means of avoiding such losses, and if this results in more funds finding their way into property, antiques, etc., this is hardly the fault of the capital market, which merely reflects conditions affecting supply of and demand for capital funds. Hence high rates of inflation can perhaps, understandably, induce funds away from productive manufacturing requirements. But one is reminded that investment in productive industry in the United Kingdom was still less *per capita* than other advanced economies when our inflation was similar or less than theirs.

While the nominal cost of capital to industry in conditions of increasing inflation is bound to increase, the demand from firms for capital is likely to diminish. In conditions of a steady *low* level of inflation, this effect may not be so serious as businesses find it possible to raise their prices as costs increase. With accelerating inflation, businesses find their costs increasing and post-tax profits decreasing, for reasons discussed in Chapter 3; in summary these are increased costs of raw materials, higher replacement costs of fixed assets, inability to raise product prices sufficiently because of price controls, reduced demand for a firm's products as government attempts to fight inflation by cutting public and private spending begin to succeed, and increased company taxation.[3]

A peculiarity associated with high rates of inflation is that although *prima facie* the cost of capital increases to unprecedented levels, the *real* cost may be negative. The real cost of redemption diminishes with inflation and the real interest rate is much less than the nominal rate, assuming that the money cost can be used

as an offset to corporation tax. It seems that in reality it is the
diminished prospect of making a profit which deters businessmen in
times of accelerating inflation. If a company fails to make a profit,
loan interest can then become a dead weight; there is then no
reduction because of corporation-tax offset, for without profits no
corporation tax will be incurred. The cost of capital may be nomin-
ally high but the market is not *causing* this, it is merely reflecting
conditions within it. (But see Chapter 5 for comments on the high
issuing costs when having recourse to the capital market.) If
institutional investors and others, banks for example, found outlets
for funds increasingly in areas other than manufacturing industry,
this is not because they had consciously chosen *not* to invest in
industry, but merely that, like any other economic entity, they take
their wares to those who want them and who will pay for them,
or they invest them in property or goods which are expected to rise
in price at a later time. Those who challenge that philosophy suggest
that the suppliers of finance should nevertheless look more as-
siduously for productive opportunities. They suggest that if more
modern equipment were available, and the environment of factory
buildings were more similar to that of office blocks (as it often is in
Japan), then long-term profitability would be more certain.

However although institutional investors were becoming comparatively more involved in gilts and property investment, as
compared with debentures and equities, in the years 1973–4, it
should not be assumed that this sort of investment is of no concern
to industry. Purchase of industrial property provides funds for
industry, for whether an institutional investor builds factories or
offices and lets them, or whether it buys them from companies and
leases them back, it is making funds available to industry. Similarly,
some of the investment in government securities may be effectively
channelled into industry, for example as funds for British Leyland's
re-equipment. But this does not fully overcome the criticism that
the institutions should be less reluctant to invest more directly in
productive industry.

Flexibility and Adaptability of the Capital Market

One measure of the effectiveness of a market is to examine its
readiness to accept and take part in change should that requirement
be identified. There have been some notable credits in this area

which include the Industrial and Commercial Finance Corporation Limited, which is the capital market's successful answer to an identified gap in its facilities (namely provision of medium-term money for companies not big enough to issue shares in the primary market). Another credit must surely be the way the euro-currency market has become centred in the United Kingdom. Also, the clearing banks' willingness to become more fully involved with medium-term loan finance has been noteworthy. There has also been some versatility in the type of financial instrument, and examples of this include the convertible debenture and types of development finance for North Sea oil which are to be remunerated on the basis of royalties from future production. There have even been occasional sorties into new methods of issue, with the offer for sale by tender an example.

Accompanying the above examples of new ideas from the private sector has been the entry of government as a versatile supplier of finance to industry. This supply takes a variety of formats: some large and new like the loans to the motor industry; some more established such as the finance made available to the National Research Development Corporation. Some of the more advanced technological industries have been well supported by government, and examples include the aircraft industry, computers and machine tools. There has been a policy for many years of providing financial assistance to areas of traditionally higher unemployment where expenditure will help to relieve that problem. Sometimes, in the last-mentioned cases, finance has been by loan, but other help has included subsidising the rate of interest on loans provided, say, by the banks, and grants. Sometimes new and controversial financial institutions have been created, and examples have been the Industrial Reorganisation Corporation (now defunct) and the National Enterprise Board.[4]

The relevant question one has to ask is whether these government activities have added to the effectiveness of the capital market, and should they be seen as a means of fulfilling a legitimate need not satisfied by the private sector, or as an example of government interference with free-market forces and/or part of the state takeover or nationalisation programme.

There are many facets involved in answering these questions, but if one measures effectiveness simply by provision of finance, then all of the quoted instances of government financial aid must have improved effectiveness. Another valid question is: were these recipients deserving of financial help because, if they were, was not the private sector likely to have supported their case? One very basic point is that if this country is to maintain the standard of living of its people, it must be able to compete internationally. This competitiveness will be eroded, and is being eroded, by the developing nations with lower wage costs and an increasing ability to take over production of what has traditionally been produced in Europe and North America. One would think that countries such as Brazil, Nigeria and South Korea might be able before very long to provide consumer durables, including cars, more cheaply than the United Kingdom. Our future must increasingly depend on more advanced technologies. But these are important areas where government has had to provide finance because of high risk and uncertainty of future profit, and consequent shortfalls from the private-sector financiers. It may well be that it is unreasonable to expect the private sector to support such industries as aircraft, computers, and machine tools more than at present. Some risks are so great that it is arguable that they should be shared by the community at large, and some industry prospects are so uncertain, due, among other things, to government mismanagement of various kinds, that one could argue that government should provide the finance and live with the effect of its actions. While modifications to the capital market will probably effect some improvements, what is really required is greater economic growth to provide the environment conducive to encouraging more modernisation, expansionary decisions, and stimulation to managers and managed.

Remedies for Slow Growth

An obvious remedy, which experience informs us is far easier to propose than to achieve in practice, is the restoration of a stable currency. Inflation discourages saving in a variety of insidious ways. Company management and shareholders may be deceived as to the true level of profits (hence the need for special inflation accounting methods). Lenders are repaid in 'debased' currency. It becomes less worthwhile to work and save as earnings and income from saving at inflated rates move recipients into higher tax brackets. Thus Professor Paish has estimated that whereas the tax rates of earned incomes of £2000 and £5000 (for a married couple with two children over 11) were 26·4 and 47·8 per cent respectively in 1950–1, they became, for the real equivalent incomes in 1974–5, 49 and 69·3 per cent respectively. The tax rates for *investment* incomes of £2000 and £5000 (for a married couple with no children) were 38·1 and 52·5 per cent respectively in 1950–1, and became 56·5 and 74·4 per cent in 1974–5. Naturally enough, those who could set aside substantial savings are deterred by such high rates of taxation, and employees earning at the lower end of the scales mentioned are concerned that the *increase* in taxation borne by them is so severe.

A corollary to this is that inflation creates unproductive jobs: to quote Professor Paish: 'whatever the level of unemployment . . . during the next few years, there seems unlikely to be much among tax consultants'.[6] It also leads, via attempts to control it, to unemployment among productive workers. A further aspect of inflation is that it encourages unproductive government spending, for the debt incurred to finance such spending (and the National Debt generally) recedes in real terms as the currency loses its value. On the other hand, to the extent that the government meets its increased expenditure by creating money, this is likely to be a *cause* of inflation rather than a consequence. Finally, although the list could be continued, inflation encourages speculative activity in the secondary market for securities, for a capital gain is one of the few ways in which those with funds to invest can keep ahead of the falling value of money – which of course gives rise to the criticism of too much attention to the short term by capital market investors.

To find a remedy to a malady one needs to know the cause. Unfortunately there is no general agreement on either cause or remedy for inflation, but a view which is well supported is that inflation is caused by prodigal monetary expansion stemming mainly from government spending in excess of taxes. Rather than meet the deficit fully by borrowing from the public and forcing up interest rates, the government effectively prints money, overheats the economy and activates the familiar cycle of wage and price rises. (An alternative explanation puts the emphasis on trade-union pressure for higher wages, which in the interests of maintaining full employment is not defused by applying very firm monetary and fiscal restraint.) If this country's inflation is greater than that abroad, there will be constant pressure on the pound, which will depreciate either steadily or in fits and starts, according to the method of exchange control in force. If, as wages increase and exports are more difficult to achieve, profit margins fall, investment and growth suffer accordingly.

Since the inauguration of the floating exchange era at the end of 1971, the United Kingdom has pursued an independent and generally more expansionary monetary policy and our level of inflation had become by 1975 well in excess of our neighbours. It follows, and current government policy now seems to be recognising this (see the Chancellor's April 1976 budget speech), that action to remedy the situation, and to encourage the industrial and commercial investment, innovation, personal initiative, willingness to work and save essential to growth, is a clear responsibility of government. The most urgent need is to overcome inflation, and here the remedy lies in the government's own hands. A halt to the printing of money to meet government deficits is essential; but if this were achieved without a cut in government spending, that is if the deficit were either met by increased borrowing direct from the public or by increasing taxes, the consequences could be damaging to business in two respects. If the government were competing for a larger share of funds from the public, interest rates could be forced up still further. On the other hand, if the government met its deficit by increased taxation, then incentives to save, work and invest would be blunted. Of the two possibilities, the former is preferable, for higher interest rates would discourage consumption and hearten savers, and more productive effort would be directed towards exports. Fortunately, the choice does not lie between these two possibilities; there is a third alternative, for the government can meet its deficit by cutting its own expenditure, thus eliminating the public-sector borrowing requirement altogether. A large cut in public expenditure could make it possible for taxes to be reduced, for more resources to be made available for that part of industry which can improve our investment and export performance. A cut in taxes and a strong movement towards a stable currency would encourage the higher level of savings which is essential if consumption is to be deferred and a higher level of investment achieved. Fundamentally, the economy, and the capital market in some respects, appear to have suffered from an excess of government activity whereas a greater government priority to control of inflation may have been wiser policy than that followed.

Given a return to stability, the capital market would reflect prices of securities which represented *real positive returns* to funds supplied rather than high nominal returns which are negative in real terms. If tax rates were not such as to discourage earnings and savings, funds would flow more readily into the market so that the real rates of return to capital can go back to the 5–10 per cent range of the 1950s and 1960s. It must be said, however, that the capital market would be no more responsible for this more orderly state of affairs than it has been for the high (but negative in real terms) rates of the early 1970s.

While the government may best promote a sound and growing economy by curtailing somewhat its own operations in the economy, this is not to say that it has not a responsibility to ensure that the market works smoothly, fairly and efficiently. Neither are we suggesting that participants within the market are entirely without responsibility for industry's lack-lustre record. There appears to be a case for some rationalisation and/or a supervisory authority for the several areas of extra-legal authority discussed in Chapter 5. Perhaps more urgently in view of the need to sharpen our competitive position among the world's industrial nations, there is a need to ensure that the market and its participants operate so as to encourage maximum efficiency and incentive to effort in every possible way. If rewards are insufficient or offered in the wrong way or to the wrong people, industry will suffer. If penalties for inefficiency or failure do not operate, industry will likewise suffer. Carefully designed share-incentive schemes can go some way towards ensuring that effort and initiative are rewarded. Profit-sharing schemes for workers could also be used to encourage co-operation rather than confrontation. It is desirable though (as discussed in Chapter 3) that top management is not too entrenched in positions of power and that they are constantly aware of their responsibility to make the best use of the different factors of production at their disposal – that is to say, that they aim to maximise profit and thereby work towards optimum efficiency. Shareholders have a role to play in supervising management. By this we do not suggest interference in day-to-day management, but a general monitoring – including initiating and approving incentive schemes, requiring the board to explain fundamental policy changes, questioning the board on important issues, ensuring that there are adequate means of securing sound management succession, and, if necessary, replacing unsuccessful top managers. Institutional investors have a responsibility in leading investors to participate in such supervision, but new legal devices should be forged whereby shrewd and competent representatives of private shareholders should also join in this supervision. There is also a need for more research to establish whether representatives of the work-force can make a valid contribution to improving profitability and efficiency by being allocated places on supervisory boards.

Inevitably, in recent years, there has been a tendency to contrast the capital-raising procedures of continental countries with those of the City. As a generalisation, capital markets are far less developed in Europe. The share of gross national income in the form of savings has been higher in leading industrial countries in Europe than in the United Kingdom, but these savings tend to flow to financial institutions and from there directly to companies rather than through the open market. In West Germany, for example, the large banks are very substantial holders of investments in many of the leading companies and play an important part in the supervision of industrial management. The banks may also vote, subject to approval, on behalf of the holders of bearer shares which have been deposited with them. Insurance companies, the federal government and the regional states also have large holdings in leading German companies.

In France and Italy the flow of funds into industry is subject to a high degree of government control. Financial intermediaries are expected to conform in their lending to the authorities investment priorities in line with national economic plans.

Some critics see the contrast between the more direct channelling of funds into industry on the Continent and the open-market method of allocating funds in the United Kingdom as pointing to the need for either the setting up of a jointly owned investment company to provide special long-term capital to industry, that is, an equity bank, and/or the provision of rediscount facilities to banks which make medium-term loans for approved, industrial investment projects. Additionally, in a similar manner to the procedure operating within the German banking system, banks in this country might issue medium-term bonds over the counter in order to raise funds for industrial investment.

Such new procedures may be helpful, and it may be thought that the French and German capital-supply methods tend to dispute claims that organisations such as the National Enterprise Board, and activities such as government direction of investment (for example into productive industries and away from property) will *per se* be inhibitors of efficient growth. But tinkering with the mechanism of the capital market is not going to solve the United Kingdom's problem of inadequate investment and sluggish growth. A fundamental overhaul of policy is required, starting with a reformed approach to fiscal and monetary controls in the hands of the government itself. Given firm government leadership to overcome inflation and restore incentives to entrepreneurs, managers, workers, risk-takers and savers, plus certain procedural reforms, the capital market can bathe in the reflected glory of a well-managed economy.

Further Reading

M. Brett, W. Brody and C. Stobart, 'The City and Industry, *Investors Chronicle* (1975).

G. J. Burgess and A. J. Webb, 'The Profits of British Industry', *Lloyds Bank Review* (April 1974).

F. Cairncross and H. McCrae, *The Second Great Crash* (London: Methuen, 1975).

P. Ferris, *Men and Money: Financial Europe Today* (Harmondsworth: Penguin, 1970).

M. Parkin, 'Where is Britain's Inflation Going', *Lloyds Bank Review* (July 1975).

P. Readman, J. Davies, J. Hoare and D. Poole, *The European Money Puzzle* (London: Michael Joseph, 1974).

J. M. Samuels, R. E. V. Groves and C. S. Goddard, *Company Finance in Europe* (Institute of Chartered Accountants, 1976).

'Capital Requirements and Industrial Finance', *Midland Bank Review* (February 1976).

Appendix

Present value of £1 tables covering
from years 1 to 15 at rates of 5 per cent to 30 per cent

Year	5	6	7	8	9	10	11	12	13
1	0·952	0·943	0·935	0·926	0·917	0·909	0·901	0·893	0·885
2	0·907	0·890	0·873	0·857	0·842	0·826	0·812	0·797	0·783
3	0·864	0·840	0·816	0·794	0·772	0·751	0·731	0·712	0·693
4	0·823	0·792	0·763	0·735	0·708	0·683	0·659	0·636	0·613
5	0·784	0·747	0·713	0·681	0·650	0·621	0·593	0·567	0·543
6	0·746	0·705	0·666	0·630	0·596	0·564	0·535	0·507	0·480
7	0·711	0·665	0·623	0·583	0·547	0·513	0·482	0·452	0·425
8	0·677	0·627	0·582	0·540	0·502	0·467	0·434	0·404	0·376
9	0·645	0·592	0·544	0·500	0·460	0·424	0·391	0·361	0·333
10	0·614	0·558	0·508	0·463	0·422	0·386	0·352	0·322	0·295
11	0·585	0·527	0·475	0·429	0·388	0·350	0·317	0·287	0·261
12	0·557	0·497	0·444	0·397	0·356	0·319	0·286	0·257	0·231
13	0·530	0·469	0·415	0·368	0·326	0·290	0·258	0·229	0·204
14	0·505	0·442	0·388	0·340	0·299	0·263	0·232	0·205	0·181
15	0·481	0·417	0·362	0·315	0·275	0·239	0·209	0·183	0·160

Year	14	15	16	17	18	19	20	21	22
1	0·877	0·870	0·862	0·855	0·847	0·840	0·833	0·826	0·820
2	0·769	0·756	0·743	0·731	0·718	0·706	0·694	0·683	0·672
3	0·675	0·658	0·641	0·624	0·609	0·593	0·579	0·564	0·551
4	0·592	0·572	0·552	.0·534	0·516	0·499	0·482	0·467	0·451
5	0·519	0·497	0·476	0·456	0·437	0·419	0·402	0·386	0·370
6	0·456	0·432	0·410	0·390	0·370	0·352	0·335	0·319	0·303
7	0·400	0·376	0·354	0·333	0·314	0·296	0·279	0·263	0·249
8	0·351	0·327	0·305	0·285	0·266	0·249	0·233	0·218	0·204
9	0·308	0·284	0·263	0·243	0·225	0·209	0·194	0·180	0·167
10	0·270	0·247	0·227	0·208	0·191	0·176	0·162	0·149	0·137
11	0·237	0·215	0·195	0·178	0·162	0·148	0·135	0·123	0·112
12	0·208	0·187	0·168	0·152	0·137	0·124	0·112	0·102	0·092
13	0·182	0·163	0·145	0·130	0·116	0·104	0·093	0·084	0·075
14	0·160	0·141	0·125	0·111	0·099	0·088	0·078	0·069	0·062
15	0·140	0·123	0·108	0·095	0·084	0·074	0·065	0·057	0·051

Year	23	24	25	26	27	28	29	30
1	0·813	0·806	0·800	0·794	0·787	0·781	0·775	0·769
2	0·661	0·650	0·640	0·630	0·620	0·610	0·601	0·592
3	0·537	0·524	0·512	0·500	0·488	0·477	0·466	0·455
4	0·437	0·423	0·410	0·397	0·384	0·373	0·361	0·350
5	0·355	0·341	0·328	0·315	0·303	0·291	0·280	0·269
6	0·289	0·275	0·262	0·250	0·238	0·227	0·217	0·207
7	0·235	0·222	0·210	0·198	0·188	0·178	0·168	0·159
8	0·191	0·179	0·168	0·157	0·148	0·139	0·130	0·123
9	0·155	0·144	0·134	0·125	0·116	0·108	0·101	0·094
10	0·126	0·116	0·107	0·099	0·092	0·085	0·078	0·073
11	0·103	0·094	0·086	0·079	0·072	0·066	0·061	0·056
12	0·083	0·076	0·069	0·062	0·057	0·052	0·047	0·043
13	0·068	0·061	0·055	0·050	0·045	0·040	0·037	0·033
14	0·055	0·049	0·044	0·039	0·035	0·032	0·028	0·025
15	0·045	0·040	0·035	0·031	0·028	0·025	0·022	0·020

Source: K. Midgley and R. G. Burns, *Business Finance and the Capital Market* (London: Macmillan, 1972).

Notes and References

Chapter 1

1. See Robin Marris, *The Economic Theory of 'Managerial Capitalism'* (London: Macmillan, 1964).

2. See generally C. S. Beed, 'The Separation of Ownership and Control', *Journal of Economic Studies* vol. 1 (1966) and M. A. Pickering, 'Shareholders' Voting Rights and Company Control', *Law Quarterly Review* (1965/248).

3. For a summary of arguments for and against the issue of non-voting shares, see the *Jenkins Report*, Cmnd. 1749 (London: H.M.S.O. 1962) p. 208. Both the Conservative government's Companies Bill of 1973 (which lapsed on the change of government in 1974) and the Labour Party Green Paper, *The Community and the Company*, Working Group of the Labour Party Industrial Policy Sub-Committee (1974) proposed the prohibition of shares with restricted voting rights.

4. See W. J. Baumol, *The Stock Exchange and Economic Efficiency* (New York: Fordham, 1965).

5. For the classic statement of this situation see A. A. Berle and G. C. Means, *The Modern Corporation and Private Property* (New York: Harcourt, 1932).

6. A typical example has been the case of Burmah Oil. In 1972 a few large shareholders attempted to gain support to limit the power of directors in their use of the very large B.P. holding of Burmah. The rebels failed to get the support of the institutions. In 1975, after the B.P. holding had been sold to the Bank of England at a third of its price of some months later, the institutions set up a committee. By then the damage had been done.

7. See generally K. Midgley, *Companies and their Shareholders – the Uneasy Relationship* (1975) and K. Midgley, 'How Much Control do Shareholders Exercise?', *Lloyds Bank Review* (October 1974).

8. The qualification requirement of most articles of large companies is not onerous, but directors' holdings are often greatly in excess of the minimum (if any) required.

9. *Abbot* v. *Philbin* [1960] 39 ATC 221.

10. The National Association of Pension Funds (in common with other institutions and private shareholders) has been concerned to ensure that schemes embody the advantages, but avoid as far as possible any potential drawbacks of the incentive principle. The Investors Protection Committee of the Association has accredited numerous schemes and no doubt made its influence felt in the drafting of regulations imposed in legislation.

11. Graham Seargeant, writing in the *Sunday Times Business News* (5 November 1972) wrote: 'insider trading is the lifeblood of the short-term trading that makes brokerage business profitable. Far from being an occasional wickedness, it is an integral part of City life.'

12. Notably by H. G. Manne, *Insider Trading and the Stock Market* (New York: The Free Press, 1966).

13. The degree of precision in terms of reward to company entrepreneurs is questionable. Also, the possibility of entrepreneurs profiting from inside knowledge of their own bad judgement raises problems; not the least of the difficulties is that, because of the weight of overriding general movements in equity prices, a piece of brilliant entrepreneurial activity will go unrewarded – the insider entrepreneur could even find himself penalised!

14. See G. D. Newbould, *Management and Merger Activity* (Liverpool: Guthstead, 1970) pp. 99–107; and B. Hindley 'Separation of Ownership and Control in the Modern Corporation', *Journal of Law and Economics*, vol. III (1) (April 1970). D. A. Singh in *Takeovers: Their Relevance to the Stock Market and the Theory of the Firm* (Cambridge University Press, 1972) found that there was a *tendency* for the profitability, growth, valuation ratio and size of firms taken over to be lower than those for firms not taken over.

15. Some companies, given the chance, might have been prepared to bid for *parts* (divisions, sub-divisions, etc.) of British Leyland.

Chapter 2

1. See also *The United Kingdom in 1980: The Hudson Report* (London: Associated Business Programmes, 1974), particularly the charts on pp. 20–1 for additional support.

2. For a discussion on these points and related aspects, see Robin Marris, *The Economic Theory of 'Managerial Capitalism'* (London: Macmillan, 1964).

3. W. Thornhill, *The Nationalised Industries: An Introduction* (London: Nelson, 1968).

4. See evidence provided by the Chartered Institute of Public Finance and Accountancy – details given in the Further Reading at the end of the chapter (p. 47).

Chapter 3

1. *The Owners of Quoted Ordinary Shares* (Cambridge University Press, 1966) and J. Moyle, *The Pattern of Ordinary Share Ownership, 1957–1970* (Cambridge University Press, 1971).

2. This sort of approach to rates of return is developed in D. Robertson, *Utility and All That* (New York: Kelly, 1952).

3. See statements for 'Sources and Users of Funds of the Personal Seeter' in recent years in *Financial Statistics*.

4. The findings were published in *How Does Britain Save?* (London Stock Exchange, 1966).

5. 'Attitudes of Private Shareholders to Mergers and Acquisitions', *Chesham Occasional Paper No. 5* (1971).

6. See Labour Party's Green Paper, *The Community and the Company* (1974) p. 18.

7. For a detailed account of information available, see R. J. Briston, *The Stock Exchange and Investment Analysis* (London: Allen & Unwin, 1975) ch. 9.

8. See generally K. Midgley, *Companies and Their Shareholders – the Uneasy Relationship* (Institute of Chartered Secretaries and Administrators, 1975) pp. 37–58.

9. Perhaps the most successful of the private shareholders' associations was Sir Julian Hodge's 'Investors' Protection Facilities Ltd'. Other successful associations have been Miss Freda Spurgeon's 'Investors and Shareholders Association Ltd' and, more recently,

Mr L. G. Harris's 'Shareholders Investment and Management Ginger Group'. See generally, Midgley, ibid. pp. 58–71.

10. For example, F. E. Brown and D. Vickers, 'Mutual Fund Portfolio Activity, Performance and Market Impact', *Journal of Finance* (May 1963); and I. Friend, M. Blume and J. Crockett, *Mutual Funds and Other Institutional Investors: a New Perspective*, Wharton Studies (1970). See also D. J. Baum and N. B. Stiles, *The Silent Partners* (Syracuse University Press, 1965). A recent U.K. study by R. Dobbins and M. J. Greenwood, 'Institutional Shareholders and Equity Market Stability', *Journal of Business Finance and Accounting* vol. 2, no. 2 (Summer 1975) concludes that U. K. institutions do not provide a stabilising influence on equity prices.

11. Dobbins and Greenwood, 'Institutional Shareholders and Equity Market Stability'. The authors found that, over twenty-eight quarters investigated, pension funds and insurance companies were net investors, throughout, unit trusts were net disposers in one of the quarters, and investment trusts were net disposers in five instances; see also Midgley, *Companies and Their Shareholders*, p. 75.

12. For details of such grants, see R. J. Ball, 'Investment Incentives', *National Westminster Bank Review* (August 1973); and 'Government Policy and the Regional Problem', a *Midland Bank Review* article (November 1975).

13. See R. D. McDougall, 'The Institutional Shareholder', *Journal of Business Finance* (Spring 1969).

14. See 'Sources of Investment Finance', *Barclays Review* (August 1974).

Chapter 4

1. See Alfred P. Sloane Jr, *My Years with General Motors* (London: Pan Piper, 1965).

2. By A. D. Bonham Carter in *Business Enterprise. Its Growth and Organisation*, ed. Ronald Edwards and Harry Townsend (London: Macmillan, 1961).

3. See J. H. Lord, 'Integration by Administration', in ibid.

4. For a brief explanation, see K. Midgley and R. G. Burns, *Business Finance and the Capital Market* 2nd edn (London: Macmillan, 1972).

5. See Robert Jones and Oliver Marriott, *Anatomy of a Merger* (London: *Pan Books*, 1970) p. 249, for a good illustration of the

variations possible. It is provided by a comment by Arnold Weinstock soon after joining G.E.C. from the smaller company Radio & Allied: 'I didn't like the decisions, especially on capital expenditure. There usually seemed to be quite inadequate information on which to base decisions.'

6. See, for example, how Jones and Marriott's researches (p. 230) reveal that, in the past at G.E.C., 'The Board of Directors played little part in deciding the policy of the company. Railing and Gamage would have lunch the day before a Board meeting and settle what to report to the rest of the Directors.' The point is also supported by Tibor Barna, *Investment and Growth Policies in British Industrial Firms*, National Institute of Economic and Social Research (Cambridge University Press, 1962) p. 32.

7. Barna, *Investment and Growth Policies in British Industrial Firms* p. 35.

8. George Walker, *The Development and Organisation at AEI* (London School of Economics, 1957).

9. Bruce R. Williams and W. P. Scott, *Investment Proposals and Decisions* (London: Allen & Unwin, 1965) pp. 18, 19.

10. For a fuller treatment, see A. J. Merrett and Allen Sykes, *Capital Budgeting and Company Finance* (London: Longmans, 1966).

11. See, for example, Bruce R. Williams and W. P. Scott, *Investment Proposals and Decisions* (London: Allen & Unwin, 1965) ch. 4.

12. *Nationalised Industries: A Review of Financial and Economic Objectives*, Cmnd. 3437 (London: H.M.S.O., 1967).

13. See, for example, H. H. Scholefield, N. S. McBain and J. Bagwell, 'The Effects of Inflation on Investment Appraisal', *Journal of Business Finance* (Summer 1973).

14. See, for example, I. Fisher, *The Theory of Interest* (New York: Macmillan, 1930).

15. See Scholefield, McBain and Bagwell, 'Effects of Inflation on Investment Appraisal'.

16. You will recall that working capital is the finance needed to keep operations going by paying for expenses, particularly labour costs, during the manufacturing period and credit period allowed to customers before goods are paid for and cash returns to the organisation.

17. There is also a very high tendency to self-financing in other countries. Peter Readman, *The European Money Puzzle* (London: Michael Joseph, 1973), reveals that from 1967–71 in France the

private sector was self-financing in the range 66–80 per cent, in West Germany the range was 64–82 per cent. The position in the United Kingdom was not significantly different; see *Financial Statistics* for particular years.

18. See Barna, *Investment and Growth Policies in British Industrial Firms*, p. 31.

19. See Alex Rubner, *The Ensnared Shareholder* (London: Macmillan 1965).

20. See J. M. Samuels and F. M. Wilkes, *Management of Company Finance* (London: Nelson, 1971) pp. 112–13 for illustrations.

21. Many of the arguments are summarised in ibid. pp. 114–16.

22. See, for example, Merrett and Sykes, *Capital Budgeting and Company Finance*.

23. A somewhat quicker approach is to use present value of annuity tables. For an explanation of this concept, see ibid.

Chapter 5

1. These are all rather specialist and outside the scope of this book. Useful comments on them will be found in *Barclays Review* (November 1972); and Jack Revell, *Changes in British Banking – the Growth of a Secondary Banking System*, Hill, Samuel Occasional Paper No. 3 (1968).

2. 'International Banking', *Guardian* (1 September 1975).

3. Many of these points, and numerous other interesting comments, can be found in Richard Spiegelberg, *The City – Power Without Accountability* (London: Blond & Briggs, 1973).

4. Ronald Grierson, 'Restoring Confidence in the City's Role', *Financial Times* (6 November 1974).

5. Ibid.

6. See P. K. Woolley, 'The Economics of the U.K. Stock Exchange', *Moorgate and Wall Street Review* (Spring 1974) for a discussion of the difficulties of measurement.

7. Table 5.1 also appears to throw doubt on the City Capital Markets Committee's view of the main function of the Stock Exchange, which it states 'is to act as a market for raising capital by issues and the cumulation of interests in capital amongst investors': see the publication *Supervision of the Securities Market* (June 1974). Perhaps this represents how the Committee would wish the Stock Exchange to be seen by outsiders.

8. See A. J. Merrett and G. D. Newbould, 'The Comparative Efficiency of Methods of Issue, *Manchester School* (January 1966).

9. Section 17 of the Act is concerned with the authorisation of unit trusts by the Board of Trade.

10. For a fuller account of incidents which have led to the development and revision of the Code, see E. Stamp and C. Marley, *Accounting Principles and the City Code* (London: Butterworth, 1970). Speigelberg, *The City – Power Without Accountability*; K. Midgley, *Companies and their Shareholders – the Uneasy Relationship* (Institute of Chartered Secretaries and Administrators, 1975); and the City Code, *Annual Reports*.

11. Christopher Marley, 'Case for a British S.E.C.', *Journal of Business Finance* (Winter 1970).

12. *The Community and the Company*, Working Group of the Labour Party Industrial Policy Sub-Committee (1974).

Chapter 6

1. J. M. Samuels and C. S. Goddard, 'Industrial Investment in Britain', *Certified Accountant* (February 1976). (See also J. M. Samuels, R. E. V. Groves and C. S. Goddard, *Company Finance in Europe* (Institute of Chartered Accountants, 1976).)

2. Ibid.

3. The general decline in post-tax rates of profit for U.K. industry has been the subject of several articles. See, for example, G. J. Burgess and A. J. Webb, 'The Profits of British Industry', *Lloyds Bank Review* (April 1974); and M. Brett, M. Brody and C. Stobart, 'The City and Industry', *Investors Chronicle* (1975).

4. See also, generally, reference to those sources in Chapter 3.

5. F. H. Paish, 'Inflation, Personal Income and Taxation', *Lloyds Bank Review* (April 1975).

6. Ibid.

Index